Praise for *The A Level Mindset*

Oakes and Griffin have produced a remarkable resource that offers a significant guide to enhancing teaching and learning at A level, but with implications beyond years 12 and 13. The resource is firstly a very practical guide to support the 'how' of effective learning as well as the 'what'. As such it provides a necessary antidote to an approach based on managing information and develops a coherent strategy to empower students' understanding and help them become confident self-managing and self-aware learners. The second important point about this resource is that it provides a model that will stimulate professional dialogue around such approaches in primary schools and years 7 to 11. The materials will also serve as a very powerful preparation for studying in higher education and employment.

Oakes and Griffin are to be congratulated and thanked for a highly practical, relevant and supportive resource.

John West-Burnham, Professor of Educational Leadership, St Mary's University College

Anyone who has ever worked with young people recognises that helping them achieve success is a complicated affair – and simply telling them to study harder rarely has the desired effect. What is special about this book is that Oakes and Griffin haven't tried to reinvent the wheel but have searched through the work of some inspirational characters whose work has implications for coaching young people. They have gathered an impressive array of gems and then packaged them into a structure which is immensely useful. Their VESPA skeleton is powerful and offers an exciting array of practical tasks that can be used to help young people. This is not a one-size-fits-all book – not every activity suits every child – the authors recognise that this is a 'pick and mix' approach to coaching. If I were still head of a school that taught A levels I would immediately order a copy for all staff teaching in that area – if it didn't teach A levels, I would probably still buy the books: some of these activities are real gems and suitable for young people of a wide age range, so much so I think I might try some myself (and it is a long time since anyone has called me young!).

Dave Harris, Business Director, Independent Thinking Limited, author and consultant

At a time when too many of us lament the way A level teaching sometimes feels like a bit of a conveyor belt, here's a book designed to give responsibility for learning back to students. It's an ingenious compilation of techniques to manage our learning in these times of information overload and endless distractions. The book is mo[re] optimistic practical approach which will help students to b[ecome] [m]anaging their studies. I learnt a great deal from *The A Leve[l ...]* of any sixth form programme.

Geoff Barton, Head Teach[er

The A Level Mindset is a book that is steeped in hard won wisdom from school leaders who have clearly grappled with supporting students at this critical stage of their education. It is a book full of practical insights and it provides an excellent framework for teachers and school leaders to help students develop their working habits. This book provides ample solutions to support students' organisation, goal setting, and much more, helping to complement our development of their subject knowledge. The VESPA framework that informs the book is well supported by interesting scholarship and there are lots of real gems of teaching strategies that can deployed in the classroom. The book is accessible, enjoyable and really got me thinking about my A level teaching.

Alex Quigley, teacher, Huntington School, author of *Teach Now! English*

This book is very obviously written by those who have had the experience (and pleasure) of working with sixth form students and the challenges that supporting them to achieve their potential brings!

The mindset approach, although based on research and theory, feels very real in the strategies and suggestions put forward. The practical and easy-to-follow strategies will support both the sixth form pastoral team, those involved in motivating the sometimes demotivated, with strategies such as the dashboard activity and 20 questions, and also the A level teacher looking for ways to strengthen resilience through practices such as The 3 R's of Habit.

I look forward to trying these techniques both in the classroom and also in more personal one-to-one intervention sessions. I strongly believe that this book will support the drive in any sixth form to raise achievement and also help develop a positive ethos which all staff can contribute to. A really positive and motivational tool for all heads of sixth form.

Caroline Lee, Head of Sixth Form and Assistant Head Teacher, Brighouse Sixth Form College

The awareness of attitude, mindset and mental toughness has risen to the top of the agenda in the world of education, particularly regarding their importance for student attainment and well-being. They make a crucial difference. However the challenge for teachers and pastoral staff is how to apply this effectively with their students.

Steve Oakes and Martin Griffin have created a first class and very practical guide to the application of these ideas in the classroom. Combining their practical experience (they have done it in the classroom themselves) and a good understanding of the theory behind their approaches, this book is a treasure trove of tools and techniques, easily adopted by teachers who want to make a difference.

Doug Strycharczyk, Managing Director, AQR

A thoroughly enjoyable book; *The A Level Mindset* has successfully integrated research and practice into an excellent user guide. It will be a valuable resource for students, teachers, parents and carers. The tools and techniques described are both workable and relevant.

Professor Peter Clough, Chair of Applied Psychology, Manchester Metropolitan University

The A Level Mindset

40 activities for transforming student commitment, motivation and productivity

Steve Oakes and Martin Griffin

Crown House Publishing Limited
www.crownhouse.co.uk

First published by
Crown House Publishing
Crown Buildings,
Bancyfelin,
Carmarthen,
Wales, SA33 5ND, UK
www.crownhouse.co.uk
and
Crown House Publishing Company LLC
PO Box 2223, Williston, VT 05495, USA
www.crownhousepublishing.com

First published 2016. Reprinted 2016 (twice), 2017.

British Library Cataloguing-in-Publication Data

A catalogue entry for this book is available from the British Library.

Print ISBN: 978-1-78583-024-2
Mobi ISBN: 978-1-78583-051-8
ePub ISBN: 978-1-78583-052-5
ePDF ISBN: 978-1-78583-053-2
LCCN 2015953353

Printed and bound in the UK by TJ International, Padstow, Cornwall

To the thousands of A level students we have had the honour of teaching and, more importantly, learning from.

To Phoebe, Max, George and Agatha; you have all of this to come.

Authors' Note

We have made every attempt to recognise the work of those who have inspired many of the ideas and concepts that we have used in this book. We would like to make particular reference to the work of Peter Clough, Carol Dweck and Angela Lee Duckworth for inspiring us to develop this system, and to thank the many students who have listened, experimented, commented, criticised and helped us tweak (and sometimes just ditch!) the tools we've developed.

Special mention must go to the staff and students of the Blue Coat School, where we have worked together for the past seven years. To Julie Hollis, an exceptional head teacher who has given us the time, space, trust and resources to design and develop this system. To Hayley Elliott and Tom Wild, who have contributed more than we could thank them for. And to our team of sixth form tutors, who've been game enough to try everything out and frank enough to give us the feedback we've needed.

The Blue Coat School is an outstanding 11–18 comprehensive school in Oldham, Greater Manchester. It is a teaching school and the lead school in the Cranmer Trust and the Northern Alliance. For more information about the school, the alliance and the trust, please visit:

www.blue-coat.oldham.sch.uk

www.northern-alliance.net

For further information: www.alevelmindset.com

For a chat: @alevelmindset

For advice, guidance, training: alevelmindset@gmail.com

Contents

Introduction

When you enter a mindset, you enter a new world. In one world – the world of fixed traits – success is about proving you're smart or talented. Validating yourself. In the other – the world of changing qualities – it's about stretching yourself to learn something new. Developing yourself. Dweck (2007), p. 14

Our story starts maybe eight years ago, in a basement office.

We were studying that summer's A level results – suffering the final stages of the journey all of us go through. It's the one that starts with sleepless nights and anxiety dreams in late July, escalates to full-blown catastrophisation by early August and ends with the anti-climax of results day which, instead of triumph or abject disaster, offers the usual mixed bag of successes and disappointments.

Picking over the grades and preparing our analysis for the head teacher that year, one fact stood out above all others. There didn't seem to be a direct link between success at the end of Year 11 and success at A level. Looking back, this sounds both a counterintuitive and, at the same time, an entirely logical observation. But at the time it seemed a significant revelation. Surely, we conjectured, those students who succeeded at the end of Year 11 continued this pathway of success and succeeded again at the end of Year 13.

Instead – and we're sure you will have experienced this – something else happened: some students made giant strides between 16 and 18, leaping up from pretty modest results in Year 11 to outstanding results in Year 13. Others went from great performance at 16 to modest grades at the end of their A level courses. There were external factors to be considered, of course, but even when we took out those young people who had fought through traumatic times, we still had vast numbers of students who seemed to hit ceilings and others who made sudden breakthroughs.

Ceiling Students and Breakthrough Students

We began the following academic year with a plan. (By which we mean a bunch of scribbled notes and a spreadsheet. We didn't get precise until much later.)

That autumn term we began to study what it was about the 'ceiling students' that made them stop progressing, and what it was about the 'breakthrough students' that made them suddenly improve. We undertook a variety of research to determine these factors. First, we identified two sample groups: a breakthrough group of students who were exceeding their target grade in the first term – this lot were seriously doing the business and getting great grades; and a ceiling group who were significantly underperforming having made a really slow start. The students of both groups were then given questionnaires, observed during lessons, had their previous academic performance evaluated, took part in focus groups and had basic data analysed. We looked at their GCSE point scores, the school they had attended to take their GCSEs, the proportion of portfolio-based level 2 qualifications, grades achieved in what we thought might be key subjects (e.g. English, maths, science), punctuality and attendance.

Here's the first point that leapt out to us: after studying the data and completing a detailed content analysis, it became clear that there wasn't a link between GCSE performance and being a breakthrough student or, indeed, a ceiling student. *Past performance didn't seem to guarantee future performance.* One group wasn't full of high GCSE achievers with glittering trophy cabinets, the other with modest achievers. The ceiling group had its fair share of students who had done very well at GCSE. The breakthrough group was a mixed bag too. There were, in short, no specific cognitive weaknesses we could find that predetermined poor performance at A level. No issue with literacy or numeracy, for example; no pattern of poor performance in a particular subject.

This ran counter to what some of our teachers were telling us, and from the kind of explanations of student performance we had heard in staffrooms across seven combined institutions over the last few years. Teachers would often explain underperformance cognitively. For example, the student was 'weak'. The student 'didn't get it'. The student 'wasn't thinking like a scientist' (or geographer or sociologist – take your pick). All-in-all, a reading of the situation that amounted to a world view best summarised by one teacher who many years ago had told us, 'In my subject, you've either got it or you haven't.'

Analysing the ceiling and breakthrough groups, it was instead the qualitative data we had collected that gave us a series of patterns – the information about students' habits, routines, attitudes and approaches to study. These seemed to be the factors which determined success. Paul Tough summarises it pretty neatly in the following observation: 'Economists refer to these as non-cognitive skills, psychologists call them personality traits, and the rest of us sometimes think of them as character' (Tough, 2013, p. 5).

At first, the specifics of character were hazy, at least to us. Detailed note taking seemed to be a factor, for example. Tidiness and organisation of learning resources seemed important too. Commitment to independent study was key, as was positivity, enthusiasm and having a goal. These all came through as characteristics and behaviours that breakthrough students had in spades and ceiling students didn't. All of this, remember, regardless of their previous performance.

To begin with we had very few ideas about what to do with this information. Because the qualitative stuff comprised observations about behaviours, it was difficult to quantify, group or categorise – and even harder to address. So we started searching for people who had discovered similar problems and worked out how to solve them.

It turned out there were plenty – and their work pointed in the same direction.

Standing on the Shoulders of Giants

There had been a huge amount of fascinating research over the previous twenty years or so, but we hadn't spent an awful lot of time studying it. Any teacher or leader working long hours with limited opportunity to dig in to academic journals and papers can find it difficult to know where to begin.

If that's you, we've chosen three major contributors who both reassured and fascinated us when we first started reading. We've arranged them chronologically below. They each offer, in their own fields, a clear, persuasive and interesting place to start. It's worth outlining some of the key aspects of their theories as they underpin many different aspects of the A Level Mindset model and provided us with the evidence, confidence and motivation to develop our own intervention programme.

Clough et al. (2002)

Peter Clough and his team work only a few miles from us at Manchester Metropolitan University, so it's fitting that we should begin with him. Clough's research on mental toughness has been adapted primarily from the sporting world, but there is growing evidence to suggest that this model can be effectively applied to education (Clough and Strycharczyk, 2014). It's something we have been lucky enough to discuss with him on a number of occasions in the recent past.

Clough makes a compelling case for mental toughness being at the heart of success and proposes a four factor model: challenge, commitment, confidence and control.

» Challenge describes an individual's view of any type of challenge. Do they see challenge as an opportunity for development or a threat?

» Commitment refers to stickability to a long-term goal.

» Confidence has two components: confidence in one's own abilities and interpersonal confidence.

» Control is also spilt into two components, emotional control and life control, and describes an individual's sense that they can regulate and influence the direction of their own life and govern their responses to intense emotion.

Clough argues that mental toughness is a malleable trait, and St Clair-Thompson et al. (2015) have shown that mentally tough students are more likely to achieve better grades, have better attendance and behaviours that demonstrate greater positivity.

In other words, it's the *study behaviours* that count. Of course, this struck a chord with us. Our own research from way back in those early days supported this view, and in the intervening period it has gone on to support it over and again.

Dweck (2007)

Carol Dweck's name is regularly spoken of nowadays, so the chances are you will know something of her work. Back then, it was pretty new to us. If it is to you, here's the gist. Her research suggests that beliefs about ability and intelligence vary greatly, and that the beliefs adopted by a young person can have a significant impact on their achievement.

She argues that individuals hold a certain 'mindset' regarding their ability. At one end of the continuum are those who believe they have a 'fixed' mindset. These individuals suppose that their intelligence is fixed at a certain point and, as a result, avoid challenging situations because they fear failure. They withdraw effort during difficult tasks to protect their ego.

At the other end of the continuum are those with a 'growth' mindset. These individuals believe that intelligence is malleable and that if you work hard you can improve your level of ability. They put themselves in challenging situations and work their way through them, listening to feedback and acting on it. They view failure as an opportunity to grow and, as a result, behave in a very different way in a learning environment.

In other words, the two types of student operate differently, study differently and think differently. Dweck's findings supported those early studies we had conducted and began to fill in some of the thinking for us.

Duckworth et al. (2007)

The work of Angela Lee Duckworth has gained significant traction since her 2013 TED talk, 'The Key to Success? Grit'. The talk has now been viewed over six million times and has promoted some interesting discussions within schools. The US Department of Education defines grit as, 'perseverance to accomplish long-term or higher-order goals in the face of challenges and setbacks, engaging the student's psychological resources, such as their academic mindsets, effortful control, and strategies and tactics' (2013: vii).

Duckworth argues that this non-cognitive trait, grit, is key to success and achievement in a number of fields, and is a stronger predicator of success than intelligence. In other words, she, like countless others, had blazed a trail for us.

Theory Into Practice

We ended that first year convinced that it was behaviours, habits and attitudes to study that were the strongest determinant of student success. Pulling apart the following year's

results, we were using fresh eyes. Here were dedicated, motivated students with good study habits – and they were the ones with the really exciting outcomes. Here were others who, despite impressive performances in Year 11, had topped out – students who were demotivated, disorganised or too easily discouraged. The positive point was that all the research we had explored told us that these mindsets, habits and behaviours could be taught.

But we had a twofold problem:

1 Our studies had shown us that a very flexible, amorphous and shifting list of characteristics were linked with success: friendship groups, grit, positivity, organisation of notes, volume of exam papers completed under timed conditions, attitude. When we hit the books again and checked with the gurus, they also mentioned a range of different qualities, all described in different ways. The most often-cited ones seemed to be:

» Perseverance, resilience and grit.

» Confidence and optimism.

» Motivation, drive and ambition.

» Tolerance and respect.

» Honesty, integrity and dignity.

» Conscientiousness, curiosity and focus.

And with these lists came extensive research to show these traits have considerable links to academic success; Snyder et al. (2012) and Weber and Ruch (2012) are good places to start if you're interested, but what we were missing was consistency. We had to make a decision about what we wanted our students to be and do, and we had to find a quick and memorable way to express it – conscious as we were that we needed a solution that was significantly simpler than the problem.

2 Having established our list, we wanted to teach these skills and behaviours in a quick, engaging and easy way. We needed to get in among the students and change their ways of thinking, behaving and working. But we couldn't find any off-the-peg, easy-to-use learning resources we could hit them with. Nothing that helpfully made a student less critical of their weaknesses, for example; nothing that made students respond to challenge more positively. If it existed at all, no one was sharing.

The Solution: VESPA

It was in attacking these problems over the next few years that the VESPA system emerged. It wasn't the first system we developed (to begin with we had a really simple model that required three things of each learner, until we realised that it lacked subtlety), but it is the best we've come up with following years of working closely with students, trying and retrying to develop a clear model. We've cut through the noise surrounding character development and suggested five behaviours and characteristics that all students need to be successful.

Our work suggests that students who are successful score highly in the following qualities:

» **VISION** – they know what they want to achieve.

» **EFFORT** – they put in many hours of proactive independent study.

» **SYSTEMS** – they organise their learning resources and their time.

» **PRACTICE** – they practise and develop their skills.

» **ATTITUDE** – they respond constructively to setbacks.

VISION

ATTITUDE

EFFORT   SYSTEMS   PRACTICE

These characteristics beat cognition hands down. We've found that ceiling students have significant gaps in one or more of these characteristics. And regardless of their academic success at 16, our studies show that these learners will hit the ceiling at A level if they don't address and strengthen those weaknesses. Conversely, students who score highly for the qualities above can and do make significant breakthroughs at A level, unlocking performance that far outstrips their target grades.

> **Students who are success seekers are not bluffed by setback, poor performance, failure or academic adversity. They take the lesson to be learnt and move on.** Martin (2010), p. 22

The VESPA Activities

In the absence of anything else out there, we've spent a number of years working on a whole series of activities that help students to develop these five qualities in themselves. Huge numbers of people have contributed their thoughts, ideas, criticisms and reflections. There are too many to name here, but we would like to thank each and every one of them for their help. This model wouldn't be what it is without them.

The first five chapters of the book cover each element of the VESPA model, giving you a series of resources to deliver under each of the headings.

The activities are designed to:

» Raise awareness about the impact a quality/characteristic can have on potential success.

» Encourage some personal reflection on the presence or absence of that quality in the student.

» Engage the student in a task that develops their practice – a reflection, discussion, coaching conversation or experiment.

Each session is designed to take fifteen to twenty minutes to complete. Many of them are flexible; they can be delivered to an individual, small groups of students, a tutor group or a whole cohort. The tasks themselves are written with a student audience in mind, so take a less formal and looser approach to referencing studies and academic journals, but we give you the details in the introduction to each section or in the teacher's notes, where we also explain how we've used the activities and what impact they've had. We've included eight tasks under each heading, giving you a total of forty to start experimenting with.

This collection isn't exhaustive. We've chosen these activities because they are among the easiest to lead and have had the biggest impact.

Using This Book

In the opening five chapters of the book, we take you through each element of the VESPA model. Each chapter follows a similar pattern: we'll introduce the element of the model and discuss some basic principles that we have discovered as we've worked with students. Many of these principles may seem self-evident but they took some time (and plenty of mistakes!) to become clear for us. Hopefully they can provide you with a shortcut to better intervention. After the basic principles, we provide teacher notes on the activities which follow. These emphasise, we hope, the flexibility of the resources but also describe the ways in which we have successfully used them. Feel free to adhere to these or ignore them – they're not precise recipes. You know your own students best.

Chapter 6 looks at how to use the VESPA model to coach students individually. One of the happy consequences of developing the VESPA model is that diagnosing student problems becomes a much speedier process. Conversations we may have found complex, challenging or circular in the past have become much easier to lead. Outcomes for individual students experiencing difficulties have become much more specific and measurable. We take you through how to use the model to interrogate issues with individual students and generate solutions.

Chapter 7 looks at the process of embedding the system across your organisation. In this chapter, we suggest some ways in which you might manage the cultural and systemic change necessary to get a team of tutors or teachers to embrace the ethos, the approach and the materials and resources associated with the A Level Mindset. The content of this chapter is drawn largely from our own practices and approaches. It is not fail-safe, of course – more an account of how you might raise awareness of the need for better character development systems and curricula, and begin the process of designing and embedding it with a team of staff.

Finally, we share ten thoughts that try to summarise the A Level Mindset. We hope these work equally well as a primer, a reminder of what it is we're collectively trying to achieve and how we can go about empowering our learners.

A Word About Our School

Context will be at the forefront of your mind as you read this, so here's the info: these tools have been developed at a comprehensive school sixth form of about 400 students. The entry requirements are five A*–C. We look for four B's – a B in each of the subjects the student wants to study. We have some students with hugely impressive GCSE results – for example, ten or eleven A* grades. We have others who come to us with some B's,

C's, D's and the odd E. All students begin four courses, and all students experience some version of the VESPA model.

At the time of writing, our Year 12 students have (as a year group) reached an ALPS grade 1 for five years on the trot. Our Year 13 students collectively score grade 2 and have done for five years (with one exception – a grade 1 a few years back. It's proved elusive since!). At the same time, we've seen rises, year on year, in high grades, A* grades, attendance and retention.

Not all of these things can be explained by the VESPA model, of course. Our students are relatively lucky: they have a hugely dedicated teaching staff, accomplished middle leaders and an impressive senior leadership team – all of these things count very much in their favour. Like any organisation, there are areas for improvement but, generally, the climate and culture is positive and aspirational.

But we did see a big jump in performance that has been consolidated since we introduced VESPA. It's quick, clear, easy to implement and we hope it could do the same for you.

1. Vision

> **When goal pursuit is fueled by personal endorsement and valuing of the goal, commitment and persistence will be high.**
> Ntoumanis et al. (2014), p. 226

What Is Vision?

We've all had those frustrating conversations that begin, 'What do you want to do with your life?' It's a difficult question to answer; indeed, some students might not be able to answer this question for many years. We don't believe that vision always has to be linked to having a clear career path. On the simplest level, it's about knowing the outcomes you want to achieve.

Our research found that students without a goal or vision hit a ceiling and underperform by about one grade. Students who don't have a clear outcome, who don't know *why* they're doing A levels, are usually the first to show decreased levels of effort when the going gets tough. Studies support this view: some researchers argue that setting a goal which is specific and challenging leads to increases in productivity (Locke and Latham, 1984).

We believe there are three parts to vision. First, it's about having a clear goal that you want to achieve. Goal setting has been used in just about every field of life – from sport to business – to improve human productivity and potential.

Second, it's about making an actionable plan. Arguably, the aspect of goal setting that is most often neglected is making a specific action plan. By breaking the goals down into sub-components and then identifying actions needed to achieve these, students are more likely to maintain motivation.

Finally, vision is about the voluntary continuation of goal-directed action. This means sticking to the goal despite any obstacles or difficulties that arise. As mentioned in the introduction, this is what Duckworth et al. (2007) call 'grit'. She found that gritty students are good at both completing tasks they are currently working on and pursuing their goals over a long period of time. It is not surprising that her research found that gritty students outperformed their peers on academic attainment. As A levels return to a linear format, the long-term stamina required to reach a directed goal will become even more important.

Dream vs. Goal

There is nothing wrong with dreams. There is probably a pretty compelling argument that says most of the great things that have ever been achieved in the world will have started as a dream rather than arrived at by accident. Dreaming is a great place to get your inspiration. But the difference between a dream and a goal is that dreams are something you just think about. To make a dream reality you have to make it a goal. And that means making a plan and taking action.

We recently worked with three underperforming Year 12 boys. When we started our coaching conversations we asked them about their goals. Two of the boys said they wanted to be professional footballers. There is nothing wrong with this dream – we were pleased they could identify and articulate it with only a little prompting. But when we started to dig a little deeper it turned out that not one of them was playing any football. Not even their local team. The closest they got to playing football was *FIFA* on the PlayStation. We'd made the mistake of thinking that if a vision could be articulated then it was legitimate. This, of course, isn't the case. It needs to be actioned and turned into a goal.

It's worth pointing out that you're not killing dreams by trying to turn them into goals, but we've found something interesting when we have these conversations – often there will be real resistance. You might hear, 'Well, actually, I don't want to do it anyway' or 'What are you hassling me for? I'm not that bothered.' Why do some students fold so easily? We think it's because what some young people tell you is what they've been telling teachers and parents and friends for a while; it's the answer they give to get someone off their case. The fact that you're taking their dream seriously is uncomfortable for them. They retreat into denial – that understandable desire to protect the ego by claiming the dream isn't important to them.

Don't be discouraged during this phase. Persist. After all, it may have been the first time anyone has seriously said to them, 'OK, how can I help you achieve this dream? What can we do to make it happen? What are the first steps?' Deciding to pursue a dream opens up the possibility of failure, so it's a frightening thing to do. It's our responsibility to understand that fear and provide a safe, non-judgemental environment.

Push vs. Pull

There are two types of goals: push and pull. Push goals have usually been set by other people – for example, parents might want their son/daughter to enter a particular career, get specific grades, choose certain courses. They then establish this push goal – which is not wholly owned by the student – and attempt to motivate them by chasing and hustling them forward. But push goals are usually only as strong as the person doing the pushing, and if they are met with resistance they often fail. Perhaps we're guilty of doing too much pushing through the GCSE years and of then removing the push at A level, thinking that students should be self-motivated.

We have to replace push with pull. Pull goals are magnetised; they're the goals that will get you out of bed in the morning. Those possibilities that are so exciting and inspiring that students almost can't stop themselves

from working towards them. Our research shows that students with pull goals are more likely to have high attendance at college, so we spend a considerable amount of time at the start of the academic year working on students' pull goals. It's helpful to identify the students with no specific goal very early in the academic year. Using some of the activities in this chapter, we've seen students make significant progress once we've started developing pull goals.

Bias Towards Action

One of the best bits of advice you can give students after a goal setting activity is to get them to identify one thing they could do today that would move them one step closer to their goal. Could they read something? Make a phone call? Book a meeting? Not taking action on a goal will lead to stagnation, comfort and failure. For every goal that a student has, they have to capture and highlight action steps. So, when coaching students on their vision there should be a relentless, optimistic focus on actionable tasks. They won't find this comfortable at first.

Teacher Guidance for Vision Activities

1. Twenty Questions

Twenty Questions is a simple, informal questionnaire, designed to stimulate discussion and reflection. The questions have been tested on hundreds of students and have been enormously successful in helping them to develop their vision. Don't think of it as a traditional questionnaire, though – this is a pick-and-choose activity where questions can be discussed, discarded, replaced, and generally monkeyed around with.

You will find that some of the questions work really well and some don't; it depends on the student you are working with. You don't have to restrict this to a one-to-one coaching session – we've had a lot of success using it on a larger scale. Below are some delivery suggestions:

» Students respond well to these questions when working with a friend. Sit them in pairs and ask one student to be the coach, the one who asks the questions and listens carefully to their partner's response, and the other the coachee. Give both students the opportunity to be the coach. Coaches have this clear remit: they must ask the question and then remain silent. Only when their partner's answer has totally petered out can they say, 'Is there anything else you'd like to add on that?' This really helps them to develop their listening skills.

» We've also used these questions as a 'getting to know you' activity. Give students the questions and ask them to pick five that they like. Then run a speed dating type activity where students sit with different people, taking turns to ask and answer the questions.

» When coaching a student one to one it can be useful to give them the twenty questions. Ask them to take the questions home and pick five they would like to discuss the next day. Give them responsibility and control over the framing of the conversation.

» We've shared these questions with parents at information evenings. Parents often say to us how hard they find these discussions and the twenty questions have provided a useful starting point for them as well as us.

It's worth pointing out that you won't get a career decision within minutes of using this activity. Instead, you're going to open up the students' thinking and give them more confidence, stir the beginnings of some awareness in them and, if it goes well, see some themes developing that might flourish when a second or third vision activity is used.

2. Getting Dreams Done

This is a quiet, reflective activity where students fill out a table with three columns, sorting and organising their hopes, dreams and aspirations into three distinct groups, depending on how much action they have taken on them.

This activity is perfect if you are working with a student who is spending too long in passive

The questions have been tested on hundreds of students and have been enormously successful in helping them to develop their vision.

daydreaming. Give them twenty-four hours to think about their responses; they can fill out the table privately at home. You don't need to see it – it's very much their property – but you will raise awareness, and then hopefully you can plan some action points into your coaching conversation. The message to the students is simple: dreams stay as dreams unless you begin to do.

3. Your 21st Birthday

This is a visioning tool where students imagine a positive point in their near future – their 21st birthday – and make notes/discuss/share what they might want to have achieved by then.

There are lots of different ways to lead this with groups of students. Some tutors might choose to start by sharing their 21st birthday experience, maybe showing some photos or talking through where they were in their lives, what they had achieved and what their hopes and dreams were at the time.

Then the students get their chance. If you're working with a confident group who are cohering well, then get them to share their hopes and ambitions with a friend. From a coaching perspective, you might want to give this activity to a student the day before you're due to meet them so they can bring some notes to the discussion. You don't need to see those notes – they are the property of the students – but ask them to discuss where

they see themselves using their reflections from the evening before.

4. Fix Your Dashboard

This activity recognises the power of visual reminders and encourages students to create a collage of pictures, quotes and other visual stimuli that can be regularly revisited when times are tough – a vision board, in essence. Our director of learning for Year 13 has used this activity to help fire up students who are struggling with motivation. She gets them to create a Word document or PowerPoint (one page/slide limit) and drop pictures of the university from which they have an offer onto the page: a photo of the campus, the halls of residence, the sports facilities/gym, the learning resource centre – whatever inspires them. She then gets them to print out the page and place it at the front of their file. Every day when they open their file they see their dashboard and are reminded why they are working so hard.

One school we worked with created A3 dashboards using images. They then had the posters printed in colour and created a display in the students' form room, so they got that everyday visual hit when tutors asked them to spend a moment looking again at their vision boards. Ask learners to include quotes, pictures of heroes, photos of siblings or parents, company or job images, material goods – anything that pulls them forward.

5. The Perfect Day

This is a free writing task where students are given a set amount of time in a safe and secure environment to record their dream day at work. This activity works well with a group.

Students are first asked to think back to their primary school days and try to remember what their dream job was back then. This can be good fun to share with the group and usually gets some interesting discussions going. The students are then given ten minutes to write their thoughts down to the questions on the activity sheet. Again, these could be shared with the group or in one-to-one discussions.

This is an activity that works well in conjunction with others – if students have a record of their responses to Twenty Questions, for example, and the following week they have a go at the Perfect Day, then some evident themes might emerge.

Days full of idle leisure aren't as unhelpful as you might think. With some probing, there are often motifs to be examined and discussed around travel, being outdoors, working in teams, celebrating successes, helping others, playing challenging games, creating fictional worlds, responding artistically to a stimulus, exercise and physical activity, companionship, leadership and many more.

If you are feeling brave, the teacher could share their perfect day. Be warned – it might have nothing to do with what you are doing now!

6. SMART Goals

This is a reflective planning activity that requires some note taking, discussion and thinking, either in a coaching situation or with a whole group of students. It works best once learners have established an overall goal because it allows you to clearly illustrate the importance of chunking steps towards a goal, building in sub-goals with deadlines, interrogating the viability of those sub-goals and refining a series of actions.

Start small. If we have an overall sense of why we're here and where we want to go, what do we need to achieve in the next fortnight? One goal per subject works well or the top five achievements that would make the fortnight great. You will find some students take to this and others might need coaching through it.

Research shows that goal setting does relate to achievement (Crust et al., 2014), but the students who are generally low on vision are, unfortunately, the ones least likely to set SMART goals, so bear that in mind and pair students so they can help each other.

7. Mental Contrasting

This tool takes the form of a grid in which students record the results of some self-analysis and reflection. It encourages learners to explore their capacity for self-sabotage by considering aspects of their habitual behaviour and elements of their own personality that are most likely to hamstring their attempts to reach a goal. It's a personal, introspective task that develops self-knowledge.

Mental contrasting is a relatively new method of goal setting, developed by Professor of Psychology at New York University, Gabriele Oettingen. She has published extensively in this area and we recommend you read her work if you would like to develop your knowledge of this technique (see Oettingen, 2014). The argument goes like this: with goal setting the goal needs to be both desirable and feasible. Mental contrasting differs from traditional methods of goal setting in that it also requires you to consider the feasibility of the goal you've set, particularly in relation to your own weaknesses. Oettingen argues that goal commitment is strengthened by the fact that you have considered the feasibility of the goal. There is some academic evidence to suggest that this method works with school children (Gollwitzer et al., 2011).

We've found that this session also works well when it's packaged as an effort activity. It can be very powerful for a student to write down the obstacles that are stopping them achieving their goal and then design a 'if … then' plan (see The Power of If … Then Thinking on page 52).

8. Fake It

Fake It is an experiment in thinking which allows a student with two competing goals to measure up both and choose between them. It requires them to block out a week of time and record their experiences in a journal, learning log or planner, then return to you for a coaching conversation.

It's an intensive activity that works best with individuals or small groups. It's not a quick fix, but it does get results, and is particularly effective with Year 13 students trapped between two possible courses at university, for example. For every goal that a student has, they should capture and highlight action steps.

1. Vision Activity: Twenty Questions

It turns out that asking, 'What is your goal?' isn't a very good way of unlocking your vision. The question is abstract and slippery and answering it is often embarrassing and frightening. But there are questions that work. Some questions get an immediate response, 'Ah! I know the answer to that!' where others don't. The following questions have been tested over and over again with students and seem to be ones that are more likely to open up some positive thinking.

We can't promise these questions will work for you; all we know is that they've worked for others. Answer these questions with reference to study and work. Try your best to practise honest and fearless thinking – that means you answer without feeling stupid or embarrassed, and you say what you feel and think. Try to write all your answers down – it really helps.

» If you could only take one subject what would it be, and why?

» What lessons or elements of study do you find easy?

» What do you do with your spare time?

» Describe an interesting lesson you had recently. Why was it interesting?

» What jobs do you avoid doing, and why?

» When does time fly? What are you doing?

» When does time seem to drag or stop? What are you doing?

» What job would you do for free?

» Who do you look up to?

» What would you try if you knew you couldn't fail?

» What puts a smile on your face?

» If you had the afternoon off to work at home, which piece of work would you choose to do?

» When you have a lot of homework, which subject do you do first?

» Describe a homework task you have recently left until the last minute or not done at all. Why?

» What do you get obsessed about?

» When you're with your friends, what do you want to talk about?

» What stresses you out?

» If you had an hour off A level work and a laptop, what would you type into a search engine?

» If you were given a small amount of money to start a company, what would it be?

» List five words you associate with 'happiness'.

2. Vision Activity: Getting Dreams Done

There is a big difference between a dream and a goal. A dream is something you imagine happening; a goal is something you take actions towards. Often, when we meet with students to discuss their vision they list their dreams, not their goals. Here is a good way of distinguishing between them.

Make a list of your hopes for the future and then put them into one of the following categories.

Pure fantasy and pipe dreams List here the things you would one day like to be or do but that you've never ever talked about. It's never been verbalised at all – it's just in your head.	
Daydreams and conversations List here the things you would one day like to be or do that you've talked about with a friend. You've admitted them and started exploring and discussing them.	
Goals List here the things you would like to do that you've taken action about. What was the action? When did you take it? What did you do when things got difficult?	

This activity will show you two key things. When your list is complete, consider the following questions:

1 What percentage of your hopes have you acted on? What chance is there of the hope becoming reality?

2 How much action have you taken? Has it been repeated, determined action? Or has it been one action taken some time ago?

What further actions can you take? What could you do to make pure fantasy and pipe dreams into goals? Success is much more to do with determination than talent.

3. Vision Activity: Your 21st Birthday

Get a pen and paper at the ready! Imagine it's your 21st birthday. You need to picture an unusual 21st at which your family and friends stand up and describe the type of person that you are for them.

Think about the following questions:

» What would you like your friends to say about you? What qualities would you like them to admire in you?

» How would you like to be described by your colleagues?

» When they list your achievements so far, what do you want them to be?

» When they describe all the things you are still going to do, and the hopes they have for your future, what will they say?

By creating a vision of what you would like to be in the near future, in different areas of your life, you often reflect the personal values that are most important to you in each of these different areas. Write down on a sheet of paper what you would like each person to say about the different areas of your life.

4. Vision Activity: Fix Your Dashboard

Imagine somebody that you admire and respect. Take your time and choose someone you look up to – often, your first thought isn't your best. Perhaps list five or ten people you admire to begin with and see what they have in common. What qualities do they have that you admire? The characteristics that you admire in others can say a lot about the type of person that you would like to be.

Take a blank piece of paper and write down the qualities of this person in each life domain: career, finance, family, personal relationships, education, qualities, activities, community citizenship and any others that you can think of.

Next, write a paragraph on the type of person that *you* would like to be in each area of your life. Practise 'no limit' thinking. Don't limit yourself by your fears, lack of money or a lack of time – clarify a vision of your ideal self.

The Dashboard

Millions of people drive to work every day. The dashboard of their car is the first thing they see on the way in and the last thing they see as they arrive home. We use the word 'dashboard' to mean what you see first thing in the morning or last thing at night. It might be the wall above your desk or next to your bedside table. It might be the wallpaper on your phone or the inside cover of your files.

We each live with a mental dashboard of people and ideas. Our research shows us that people who have even a brief reminder of a positive role model – from looking at their dashboard – have hugely increased levels of motivation.

We have also worked with students who have altered their dashboards. One student put a photograph of the university she wanted to go to inside her file, so she saw it each time she opened it up to work. Another student covered his bedroom wall with inspiring quotes and messages. Another listed all the people who would feel proud and excited if she did really well, and stared at those names before each revision session. For further information on this, check out Dan Coyle's brilliant guide, *The Little Book of Talent* (2012), which encourages people to study the person you want to become.

Try a dashboard display of your own!

5. Vision Activity: The Perfect Day

Every primary school child in the country will be able to tell you what they want to be. Why? Because at that age teachers encourage children to express their hopes and dreams in writing activities with titles like, 'When I grow up …' Look in your old school books and you will find you've done this too.

But no one asks teenagers to write about what they want to be. It's as if, by this age, we're embarrassed to have hopes and dreams. We shouldn't be. *Having hopes and dreams is more important at this age than at any other time of life.*

So, put your headphones in, get some music on and write without shame. It will be like the old days! Here are some questions to help get you thinking. Your task is to have a go at describing your perfect day at work to help you develop a long-term vision.

» Are you working indoors or outdoors?

» Do you work at home or away from home?

» Who are you with?

» Are you leading a team? Part of a team? Alone?

» When do you start or finish?

» What are you wearing?

» What is your workspace like?

6. Vision Activity: SMART Goals

In this goal setting activity you are going to develop SMART goals – that is, something concrete and doable which will help you reach your goal. SMART goals are a proven method of maximising goal setting success.

Pick one of your goals. Whether you choose an education goal, a career goal or a personal goal, try to identify how you can make your goal SMART:

» **Specific.** Be as precise as you can rather than general.

» **Measurable.** How will you know when you've reached your goal? Write: 'I will know I have achieved my goal because …'

» **Action-based.** What can you do to get the goal started? How? What's step one, step two, step three and so on?

» **Realistic.** Has someone done it before? Could you speak to that person? Is there evidence to suggest that you can do it? What previous personal successes are connected to your goal?

» **Time-bound.** When do you want to do this by? Avoid, 'One day I'm going to …'; instead be much more precise.

Use the template below to record your SMART goals.

Specific	
Measurable	
Action-based	
Realistic	
Time-bound	

Short-Term SMARTs

SMART goals take your goal setting to the next level but they need practice. Try setting four or five SMART goals for the next fortnight. Imagine how you would feel if you had every one of those five short-term goals done in the next ten working days! You might want to choose one per – for example:

» A homework piece you want to complete really well.

» A part-time job application and interview you want to go smoothly.

» An upcoming test you want to perform well in.

» A section of notes you want to reorganise and revise.

7. Vision Activity: Mental Contrasting

This is a positive thinking exercise that helps you define your vision. In her book, *Rethinking Positive Thinking* (2014), Gabrielle Oettingen argues that too much positive visualisation can rob a person of their desire to succeed – they get happy enough just dreaming about something and never end up doing it. Any goal you set will usually have obstacles in the way of you achieving them (if they were easy everyone would be able to achieve them!).

Mental contrasting gets you to think about these obstacles and develop a 'if … then' plan to help you overcome them. The process also gets you thinking about the feasibility of your goals. If you can't formulate an if … then plan, then your goal might not be possible at all!

Here's how it works:

1. WISH

Spend a minute or two thinking in detail about something you want to accomplish. (For example, this could be the grade you want to achieve in a particular subject.)

2. OUTCOME

Vividly imagine the best thing you associate with having achieved that outcome. (That 'best thing' might be anything related to the outcome. It might mean getting into the university of your dreams!)

3. OBSTACLE

Ask yourself what internal obstacles are most likely to get in the way. (That weakness inside you that holds you back from higher grades or a better exam performance.)

4. PLAN

Formulate an if … then plan for what you will do when that obstacle arises. ('If I find myself checking Twitter, Facebook or going on Netflix, I'll get up immediately and turn off the Wi-Fi.')

8. Vision Activity: Fake It

Sometimes it feels almost impossible to make a decision. We've worked with lots of students who are torn between two or more goals. They can't decide between the two, three or even four options they've got. If this is the case for you, we have a solution – the 'fake it' method. Here's how it works:

Week 1

Choose one of your options. It might be applying to university to study geology, getting a business and management apprenticeship or taking a gap year.

For a whole week, you're going to pretend that you've made your decision; that the option you've chosen for the week is what you want to do with your life more than anything else. The burden of having to make a decision is gone – you've made the decision. You're not allowed to think about the other options at all for the whole week.

In pretending you've already made your decision, do the following:

» Research the option – find out all you can about it.

» Get excited about it. What's on the course? How much will you earn on this apprenticeship? What are the career prospects afterwards? Who else among the people you know has chosen that option? Why are they choosing it? What is making them excited?

On Friday, make a note of the way the week has made you feel. Has it been a good week? Discuss it with a friend or a tutor.

Week 2

Choose another one of your options. (Not the week one option – you're ditching that.) Now, you're going to pretend that this is your decision. Repeat the process above.

Compare and contrast:

» Which was the better week?   » Which was more enjoyable?

» Which made you feel more excited?   » Which felt more like you?

Spend time with a teacher, tutor or friend explaining your responses.

2. Effort

What Is Effort?

The effort section of the VESPA model refers to how much hard work you do. Before we look into ideas about effort further, however, it's worth remembering that fixed mindset learners carry with them the myth of effortless success. That's half your students and half your staff thinking, 'You've either got it or you haven't. If you've got it, superb work arrives effortlessly; you're blessed with the right genetic code and life's a breeze. If you haven't, you have to work really hard. It's slow and painful, which is a clear indication that you haven't got what it takes.'

A good place to start is by promoting stories, studies and research which compel fixed

mindset learners to think again. You might share with them that effort is 'a function of the intensity, direction, and duration of one's exertions toward a goal' (Duckworth et al., 2007, p. 1098), or that Bloom (1985, p. 54), who conducted a study of world class performers in a variety of disciplines, noted that the discipline and 'willingness to put in great amounts of time and effort' were significant factors in success.

Measuring Effort

In order to effectively measure, encourage and model high levels of effort, first you have to quantify it in a way that unifies everyone's thinking and in a way that everyone can understand. A simple enough model to measure effort is to do it in hours of independent study per week. This work can include homework, research, wider reading, consolidation of previous learning, revision, preparation for tests and so on. The specific actions to be undertaken come later – that's covered by the practice element of the model – but the time itself is a measure of effort.

Once the meaning of effort in terms of independent study has been clearly established, two further things are possible: (1) you can define what independent study is, and (2) you can ask students how many hours of it per week they are doing, and use this to inform your intervention.

We've found it useful to think of independent study as falling broadly into two camps: reactive and proactive.

Reactive independent study involves completing tasks set by teachers and should only form a small proportion of a successful student's time. In the early stages of Key Stage 5 study, some young people understandably assume that their job is entirely reactive – after all, it has largely been so at Key Stage 4. They react in response to tasks set by the teacher in the lesson. Reactive students have a list of jobs to do; they complete those jobs and then stop.

They might view a teacher's request for further independent study with confusion or bewilderment. 'What do you mean?' they might say, 'I'm caught up with all my homework.' Study means 'catching up' and 'keeping up' with a teacher; responding to a series of tasks and challenges.

Proactive independent study is, put simply, work students set themselves. Asking a student, 'How much work do you set yourself?' or 'When did you last set yourself a piece of work?' is a quick and effective way to assess their capacity or readiness for proactive independent study. It looks different for different subjects, but it's the scientist who reviews each lesson's notes alongside the relevant chapter from the course textbook, it's the government and politics student who keeps a folder of current affairs news items and it's the linguist who watches target-language movies for fun.

Proactive independent study is teachable, but students not used to it need some first steps to get them started. A reactive student told to 'read around their subject' will be understandably nonplussed. Create a proactive study checklist of ten activities for your A level course, then ask your students to tick them off as they try them out. Cynics and pedants will tell you it's not 'independent study' if you've told them to do it, but you're creating a culture in which learners understand what proactive study looks like, you're giving them space to experiment with new ways of learning and you're investing in their cultural capital. They will be doing it without your support soon enough.

To conclude, if you're clear on what proactive, effective independent study looks like, then you can begin to reasonably demand it of your students.

Understanding the Need to Belong

We discovered something that seems ridiculously obvious in hindsight, but it took us ages to realise. If you ask students how much effort they're putting in, unless you've quantified and defined 'effort', they can't give you a useful answer. We used to ask them to rate their effort on a scale of 1–10, but everyone gravitated towards 6. The students putting in the least effort scored themselves at 6. Some of our hardest working students also scored themselves 6. They were making a subjective judgement based on what they thought was 'average' or 'normal', and they took that reading from their peers. That's because students surround themselves with similar people. They feed the need to belong by normalising whatever level of effort they are putting in.

Here's how to crack this one. Interview your highest achieving students using a questionnaire and ask them how many hours per week of independent study they've done in order to achieve their wonderful grades. Gather together as much data as possible when talking to them. Then do the same for your lowest achieving students.

Now you've got data to share with every student. In our organisation, we found that our highest achieving students were putting more effort into their studies and committing more hours per week than the others. The figure for Year 12 was twenty hours per week for the very best students. Our least effective learners gave us a figure of three hours per week. We repeated the process for groups of learners across cohorts. Everyone in Year 12, year after year, fell between three and twenty hours per week (in Year 13, we got five and thirty as our two extremities).

Try it yourself. By doing this, you remove the students' opportunity to normalise their levels of effort. Without knowledge of these figures, students can tell themselves, their parents and their teachers fictional stories about the amount of effort they are putting in. They surround themselves with similar students putting in similar levels of effort and report that 'No one else is doing any independent study either' or 'No one does the amount of work the teachers recommend'. But if everyone knows that top performing students put in twenty hours per week, for example, there is no hiding.

You also standardise expectations about effort. Instead of mixed messages from different teachers in different departments, you get one clear headline figure. Gone is the experience of the student who, at the end of the first half-term has been told, variously: 'Do four hours of study a week in my subject', or 'Do eight hours of portfolio work a week in my subject', or 'For every hour I teach you in my subject, give me an hour of independent study back' or 'Just do a good amount of reading in my subject'. Instead, everyone hears the same song: top performers do twenty hours per week.

Using the key principles above, you can arrive at a point where every student understands that:

» Success requires large amounts of effort.

» Effort is measured in hours per week of independent study.

» Independent study is a proactive process.

» Top performing students commit X hours per week to their studies.

Then you're *really* ready to get the best out of your learners.

Comfort Zones

There is one final piece of the jigsaw. You can't ask someone to run a marathon without having first developed distance running over a series of shorter outings. The year we told every student about the twenty hours per week rule on the first day of term, we created some real crises. Students saw it as impossible; it was too far away from their zone of comfort and their current way of working.

So, our final recommendation for building effort is that you graduate the levels of effort required by your students. Set an eight hours per week target in the first half-term. Raise it to ten or twelve in the second, then up again in the third. We use half-term four as the point at which twenty hours per week is recommended.

One final thing: effort is a habit. What seems impossible can quickly become the new normal. Part of building high levels of effort in students is about improving their productive independent study habits. You will see this approach reflected in the material that follows.

If you ask students how much effort they're putting in, unless you've quantified and defined 'effort', they can't give you a useful answer.

Students surround themselves with similar people. They feed the need to belong by normalising whatever level of effort they are putting in.

Teacher Guidance for Effort Activities

9. The 1–10 Scale

This is a self-evaluation activity for students so they can rate themselves in terms of their effort, choosing a score between 1 and 10.

They are presented with a scale running from 1 to 10, with 'low levels of effort' and 'high levels of effort' as the descriptors. They are then asked to give themselves a score – usually inflated! – which represents their level of effort. They then see the same scale but this time the descriptors are replaced by numbers of hours per week spent on independent study, so 'low' becomes three hours per week and 'high' becomes twenty hours per week. When they estimate a second time, responding to this new information, they quickly adjust their effort estimation downwards!

This is our starting point for an effort activity. We've done this with hundreds of students together in a lecture hall. We asked them to hold in their head the number they would award themselves using the first scale, then adjust that number once they had seen the actual measurements on the scale. You can also do it with a class, a small group or an individual.

A rough rule of thumb is that students will add three hours per week to their total if they're talking with you one to one. It's that very human need to belong – they know what you want to hear and they will cleave towards it. So, if a student is telling you they're doing three hours per week, read that as nothing at all.

When working one to one, particularly with kids who aren't working hard enough, we inevitably spend some time digging into exactly when those hours are completed. Take out a timetable with their study periods on and ask them to outline precisely what happened in the last week. As you draw up the results, get students to be as specific as possible by asking:

» 'What do you do in that hour?' This question tells you whether the student is reactive or proactive in their approach.

» 'Where did you work?' This gives you a clear sense of their underlying motivations. The space they choose tells you how much they subconsciously want to be disturbed (see Recognising Your Blockers below).

» 'Who did you work with?' This gauges something about character and study preference.

» 'Of the hour you spent, can you estimate how much of it was in-the-zone, concentrated and focused work?' If you can get students to be honest here, then you can get them to change. Commonly, we'll get 'Thirty minutes' as an answer. Students working surrounded by others are 50% less productive than their counterparts in a silent study area.

Step up the targets week by week. Use a list of proactive independent learning strategies if the student claims they have 'nothing to do'. Perhaps, more obviously, find out whether your teaching staff are setting enough work.

10. Working Weeks

This is a hand-out which presents students with the average working weeks in Europe, measured in hours per week, followed by some information gathered about senior leaders and CEOs and their working weeks. There is some information for the students to read through, then a discussion and some questions for them to answer; the aim is to get them thinking about their own working week relative to others.

We use this activity in large groups – it's another one we've done en masse with hundreds at once – but it can be followed up in tutor groups or smaller teams. A good place to start is by discussing your own working week; this is useful for students to listen in to and then share thoughts, ideas and experiences. 'What do your parents do for a living?' and 'What are their weeks like?' are also good places to start. Ask about aunties and uncles, older brothers and sisters – get a conversation going about the work–life balance and assemble the observations. The key thing to remember is that an A level student will be on something like a twenty to twenty-four hour working week (excluding study periods). There is a big gap between what they do and a steady 9 to 5 job, and the aim of this activity is to encourage students to see their week with more perspective and to adjust their effort levels accordingly.

Try encouraging a 9 to 5 culture with some students. Their home circumstances might mean work there is difficult, either because of a lack of resources and space or an excess of it. Instead, students can raise effort levels significantly by working before and after school, and still have their evenings free.

The vast majority of students have part-time jobs. Get a college-wide agreement on how many hours of paid work are too many and communicate that to students and parents. (In our school, ten hours of paid work a week is the maximum recommended.) For more on working patterns, check out Blaire Palmer's *The Recipe for Success* (2009).

11. The Three R's of Habit

This is a planning activity which requires students to design a new habit they want to begin – an effort habit. It gives them the framework for designing a new habit and can, a week or so later, lead to a coaching conversation in which learners report back on their habit experiment.

It is adapted from Charles Duhigg's excellent book, *The Power of Habit* (2014). Thinking in terms of habit loops helps to break a mindset you will often hear expressed by students and staff – the notion of 'laziness'. We find this term unhelpful. It's far too easy a catch-all for explaining poor performance. Reframe that thinking in terms of habit. Students aren't lazy, but they may have developed habits and patterns of behaviour which preclude them from putting in large amounts of effort. The job of the organisation is to encourage learners to form new and more positive habit loops.

Avoid also the language of 'bad habits'. We don't want learners psychologically equating low levels of effort – which we can solve quickly – with say, smoking. Low levels of effort are not *that* addictive! Instead, use the language of creating new habits rather than breaking old ones. The former is much more positive, empowering and exciting. Make sure the habit takes place outside the classroom, not inside. This is not about better classroom behaviour but about encouraging proactive independent study.

Finally, make sure you set a habit target that is very easy to achieve to begin with. To embed a new habit, it's actually got to happen five, ten or twenty times on the trot. You don't want a student failing to execute their new habit at any point. With that in mind, choose 'A twenty minute review of progress in subject A' as a target, as opposed to 'An hour's intensive revision'. Five days later, when you're meeting to review progress, a student with the first target has done 100 minutes of proactive independent study and is gathering momentum. Meanwhile, the second student may well have done the first hour but couldn't face it after that and stopped.

12. Recognising Your Blockers

This is a coaching tool that frames a ten or fifteen minute discussion with a student. The resource describes a series of behaviours and then requires learners to explore the extent to which their behaviours are similar. We've found it's a good one if you want to encourage that 'Aha!' moment in a student. It's best used as a coaching activity with a learner who is finding it difficult to form new habits because of long established subconscious psychological tricks. You might well recognise yourself in this one too – we really are our own worst enemies!

13. Frogs and Banisters

A procrastination-busting written task in which students take stock of the kinds of tasks they are doing with their time. They will need to generate a long list of tasks, homework and projects they're working on, but also all the other things they're doing to fill their time. They have to then categorise the activities.

What you're looking for are the useful or important activities they're deliberately avoiding or putting off, and the less useful tasks and activities they're engaged in instead. You might find this helpful for refining and tweaking effort habits. We use this activity when we coach students who are showing real potential in terms of hours per week but aren't yet reaping the rewards.

Part of procrastination is finding and completing jobs that don't need doing, and this activity encourages students to explore that idea. Give them some help by sharing a weakness of your own at this point. For example, we've both displayed classic symptoms in the past; we couldn't start an essay until we had rearranged all our notes, highlighted all the key information and then copied it all out again. As university students, we were both experts at selecting any comfortable job which didn't require us to face down the challenge of a more important task.

Time is our most important currency. It's non-renewable! If we lose this hour we never get it back. This audit can give students a clear sense of what they're doing – and a commitment to shift away from banisters and towards frogs.

14. The Ten Minute Rule

This is a quick-fix activity to challenge the fear of starting something. The student needs a piece of work that they're avoiding, a quiet room and a member of staff to keep an eye on them. We've used it as a speedy habit formation solution, and it is similar to the Three R's of Habit. It can be executed so speedily that you can ask the student to do it in your presence. Sometimes the hardest thing is just *starting*. But once you've started enough times, the fear disappears.

15. Inner Storytelling

This is a reflective planning activity where the student(s) choose a mantra for the week ahead, and repeat it as often as they can in order to change the potentially negative narrative they have about themselves. It works well as a coaching tool with one or two students, perhaps a small group at the most.

There are suggestions for mantras that students might want to adopt, and some explanation of why choosing and repeating a mantra might be useful, but the success of this activity comes from the ownership students have over it. For this reason, it's quite a personal task which learners might want to complete alone or away from school or college.

16. The Power of If ... Then Thinking

This is a planning tool for students to scope out and plan a small project or challenge – perhaps a piece of homework, coursework or revision – and anticipate the kinds of events that might sabotage or derail it. We've found it a great tool for using with procrastinators!

It works well in conjunction with Recognising Your Blockers (page 46) and Mental Contrasting (page 28). We've got the best out of it in one-to-one coaching situations because you're asking a student to share their psychological blockers – those personal thought patterns that short-circuit their attempts to do the right thing.

Graduate the levels of effort required by your students. Set an eight hours per week target in the first half-term. Raise it to ten or twelve in the second, then up again in the third.

9. Effort Activity: The 1–10 Scale

On a scale of one to ten

1   2   3   4   5   6   7   8   9   10

Look back at the work you've done so far this term and think about the levels of effort you've put in to your studies. Use the scale above and the following guideline to choose your number:

» **1:** Little or no effort.

» **5:** Some effort – you're working quite hard.

» **10:** High levels of effort – the hardest you've worked.

Be honest with yourself and choose your number.

What Are Other Students Doing?

The problem with making a judgement about your own levels of effort is that scales can be subjective. Here are some of the issues:

» The numbers mean different things to different people.

» Students tend to surround themselves with people who do either similar or less work than they do. This means they 'normalise' the amount of work they are doing, even feel good about it, because they can point to someone doing less than they are.

» Students don't have a clear idea of what the hardest working students are doing.

» No one can know what students are doing in other schools and colleges.

The answer is to get some concrete figures so the choice of number is a more accurate reflection of your levels of effort relative to other students.

Take another look at the 1–10 scale.

On a scale of one to ten

1   2   3   4   5   6   7   8   9   10

Look back at the work you've done so far this term and think about the amount of effort that you've put into your studies. Use the scale above and the following guidelines to choose your number:

» **1:** 0–2 hours' independent study a week.

» **5:** 10 hours' independent study a week.

» **10:** 20 hours' independent study a week.

Be honest with yourself and choose your number.

We got these hourly figures by interviewing students, so we know that AS level students who end up with three A's tend to do twenty hours of independent study a week. Questionnaire results show that the twenty hours tend to be spread across four subjects and equates to about four or five hours per subject per week outside of class. When we do the same with A level students, top students (those aiming for three A's or A*'s) do about thirty hours of independent study per week.

What Can You Do?

First, reach 5/10. That means putting a timetable in place that takes you to ten hours of independent study per week. With your tutor, plan what that will look like and go with it for a period of time. Studies say it takes thirty days to establish a habit. Make ten hours a week your habit for a month.

Then, in consultation with your tutors or teachers, step it up gradually. Go for twelve hours next, then fourteen. If you're doing twenty hours a week by the spring of AS or A2, you're in a really good place.

10. Effort Activity: Working Weeks

In *The Recipe for Success* (2009), journalist and author Blaire Palmer interviewed hundreds of high earners and pulled together the qualities she found. There are, she reckons, ten key characteristics to success. She calls the tenth 'graft', by which she means just putting in the hours.

How Long Are the Working Weeks of High Earners in the UK?

As a student who takes all study periods as frees, you're on about twenty-three hours a week.

As a student who works all your frees, you're doing thirty-five hours a week.

A 9 to 5 working week amounts to forty hours a week.

The average UK worker does forty-three hours a week.

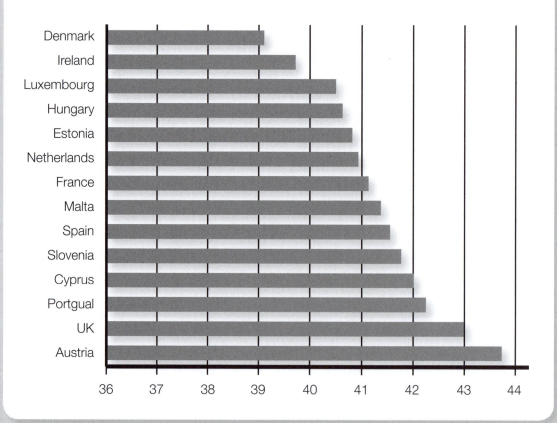

The government recommends a maximum working week of forty-eight hours.

High earners (top tax bracket of over £50K a year) average fifty hours a week.

Company bosses interviewed worked between sixty and eighty hours a week.

What Does a Working Week Like That Look Like?

A fifty hour working week is …

Start each day at:	Take a lunch break from/to:	Go home at:

An eighty hour working week is …

Start each day at:	Take a lunch break from/to:	Go home at:

Review Your Working Week

How many hours are you putting in? How do you compare to your parents, or to the average UK worker? Plan where you could get some extra hours from.

11. Effort Activity: The Three R's of Habit

Stanford University has a Persuasive Technology Lab. Here, academics study how interactive technology is changing our habits. Its founder and director, Dr B. J. Fogg, is studying how mobile phone technology – apps and so on – can develop habit formation. Effort is also a habit. The level of effort you put into your study is a result of your habits. Some people have got the effort habit, some people haven't.

The argument goes that there are three elements to habit formation, often referred to as the three R's:

» **The reminder.** This could be a feeling, a place or a time of day – it's your body or brain giving you a trigger that initiates the behaviour. It might be getting some chocolate, going home early or putting away the work you know you should be completing.

» **The routine.** This is the behaviour itself. Going to the canteen and buying the chocolate or taking the bus home instead of staying on to do some studying. Often people will feel a twinge of guilt during the routine but do it anyway.

» **The reward.** This is the good feeling you get – the benefit you gain from engaging in the behaviour. It might not last long but it is a tempting prospect.

If you haven't currently got into the effort habit, how can you go about changing? You can use the three R's in your favour. Rather than thinking about stopping old habits – which is a mistake many people make when 'giving up' something – the trick is to think of it as starting a new habit. This means you will need a new reminder to trigger your new habit, a new routine to go through and, best of all, a new reward to give yourself!

How To Do It

» Choose a trigger attached to something that happens to you every day. For example, 'At the end of every lunch hour I will …', 'As I finish my breakfast I will …', 'As the bell for the end of the college day goes, I will …' or 'At the end of the 6 o'clock news I will …' Think about and discuss with your tutor what your trigger might be.

» Choose a routine that is easy to achieve. It might be to sort out your notes for thirty minutes, review the homework you've been set for thirty minutes or do one hour's work on a difficult A level. The key thing is this: in the beginning, performance doesn't matter. Routine matters.

» Finally, the reward. Start small with a verbal reward. It might be a 'Good work!' spoken aloud to yourself, a short period of time doing something you enjoy or a cup of coffee.

12. Effort Activity: Recognising Your Blockers

A 'blocker' is a psychological barrier that stops you working. It might be a pattern of thinking or a habit you've established that you can't break. All of us have blockers – thoughts and feelings that stop us doing the thing we know we really need to do.

To put in the effort for A level success you have to recognise your blockers and break down those patterns of thought. This four stage model is useful for recognising the behaviours and thought patterns that are a sign of blockers.

1. Initial Lack of Motivation

Everyone feels discouraged at some point – the feeling that they don't want to complete a piece of work, finish an essay or put in a couple of hours on a tricky piece of coursework. The difference is what you tend to do next …

2. Bypassing Conscience

Most people will feel guilty when they don't work ('I should be finishing that essay …'), but sometimes we find ways of bypassing our conscience. We deliberately rethink the situation until we feel better about it. Some thought patterns you might have include:

» Student A hasn't done it either, so I'm not that bad.

» At other schools/colleges they don't even do this piece, so why should I?

» The instructions were unclear, so I've got an excuse. I'm telling myself I didn't really understand.

» I rushed a piece last time and the grade was OK. I'll do that again.

» I deserve a break. I've always really loved this TV programme – I'll watch it instead.

» I'm going to do something else that has some 'educational value'.

3. Creating An Opportunity

Next, there needs to be something nearby that can distract you. Some students work near others and tell themselves this is beneficial because they can ask for help if they need it.

What they might actually be doing is hoping for a distraction to occur. The same goes for workspaces. Do you work near or next to your phone, laptop, tablet, PS4 console or TV, secretly hoping for something to take you away from your work? If this is you, then you are subconsciously (or maybe deliberately!) creating the opportunity for blocks to occur.

4. Getting Away With It

Finally, for the pattern to continue, you need to feel that you have got away with it. The thought pattern here often goes, 'Nobody said anything, so it must be alright' or 'I didn't get told off, so I'll do it again.'

This activity might help you recognise your own tendency to self-sabotage. Don't worry, everyone does it to a certain extent – really productive people have learned to fight the feeling!

Once you've noticed the ways in which your blockers get in the way, try the following:

» Think about a piece of work you never completed. How did you justify the non-completion to yourself? Which task on your list at the moment are you least likely to do? Why?

» Take a task that has been on your to-do list for a while because you've been putting it off. Why is it there? Is there an action you can take right away which will make the task suddenly achievable?

» Next time you put a task off, ask yourself why. Are you simply sequencing tasks and saving it for later? Or is this an act of self-sabotage?

The response: if you feel self-sabotage coming on, move location. Get yourself to a quiet room, a study area or the library. Start the task. You don't even have to finish it – work for thirty minutes or so – but get it started. You're less likely to sabotage a project that is already underway!

'If you have to eat two frogs, eat the ugliest one first'

13. Effort Activity: Frogs and Banisters

This activity focuses on the separate advice of two academics. The 'frogs' part of this advice comes from time management guru Brian Tracy, who in *Eat That Frog!* (2013) asks his readers to imagine that tasks are frogs you have to eat. He chooses this metaphor because the thought of such tasks is often very off-putting. His advice is as follows: 'If you have to eat two frogs, eat the ugliest one first' (p. 2).

This is another way of saying that if you have important tasks to apply your effort to, start with the biggest, hardest and most important one first. This is related to Tim Ferriss' idea of the 'lead domino' (which he talks about in his podcast 'How to Build a Large Audience From Scratch (And More)' at http://fourhourworkweek.com): if you do the tough tasks first, your effort will be worthwhile because it will pay dividends later. So, list all your frog tasks – in order of ugliness!

The 'banisters' part comes from computer science professor Randy Pausch. 'It doesn't matter how well you polish the underside of the banister,' says Pausch (2010, p. 108). In other words, don't worry about unimportant details – put your effort where the result will be greatest.

List the work you've done recently. Have you been eating ugly frogs (getting tough, important jobs done) or have you been polishing the underside of the banister (half-heartedly completing easier looking jobs that aren't really important)?

Frogs	Banisters

Which jobs are you doing that you can stop? Which jobs are you avoiding that you should tackle?

14. Effort Activity: The Ten Minute Rule

If you are in a position where you are regularly putting up barriers to work, the Ten Minute Rule is a good way of breaking them down. What do we mean by 'barriers'? Many students will avoid A level classwork or homework because it is hard. Instead they will:

» Do something more comfortable but less useful. They might copy out some notes or make a mind-map when really they know they should be doing the exam paper their teacher has set them under timed conditions.

» Claim that homework or independent work 'isn't realistic' as a way of avoiding it. ('This is pointless. The real exam will be totally different so why bother?')

» Get into a deep discussion about something related so they feel like they are working.

» Look for someone else who isn't doing it. Or in extreme cases, tell themselves that no one is doing it.

You may recognise these behaviours in yourself and others – putting up barriers to independent work to avoid it.

If this is you, the Ten Minute Rule is a good way to break through barriers. It's very simple:

1 Tell yourself you are going to do ten minutes of intense work. That's all.

2 Decide what work the ten minutes is going to be spent on.

3 Clear a space and sit down with the right materials to hand.

4 Start.

You can, of course, stop after ten minutes. Even if you do, you've done ten minutes more work than you would have done. But what often happens is that ten minutes becomes twenty. Sometimes even half an hour or longer.

What do we learn from this experiment? Hopefully, you will realise that the thought of work is often much worse than the work itself.

15. Effort Activity: Inner Storytelling

In *Better Than Before: Mastering the Habits of Our Everyday Lives* (2015), Gretchen Rubin, a lawyer and writer, says that the language we use to describe ourselves – our 'inner storytelling' – massively influences the amount of effort we put into a project.

Rubin argues that 'we tend to believe what we hear ourselves say, and the way we describe ourselves influences our view of identity' (2015, p. 225). Perhaps this describes you – maybe you've told yourself these stories for years? Inner storytelling helps us live up to our own hopes and fears.

For a week, your challenge is to change your inner storytelling. This, in turn, could well change your patterns of behaviour, your habits and, ultimately, the effort you put into your work. A good place to start would be to choose one of the following stories to tell about yourself:

» When I started A levels, I suddenly became a hard-worker. I battle.

» I give 100% whatever I do. I never give up.

» When I say I'll do something, I do it.

» I'll deliver. I always do.

» I don't waste time. I get things done.

» I'm dedicated and strong under pressure. People can rely on me.

» When there is a challenging task, I go at it until I'm done.

» I'm not lazy or flaky. I'm no shirker.

Once you've chosen your new story, you need to find a method of verbalising it. The word 'mantra' is often used to describe an utterance or phrase with psychological power. This is what you're creating here. Find a time of day when you can repeat your mantra – on the bus, in the shower, walking home or crossing the campus between lessons. Then try it for a week.

16. Effort Activity: The Power of If … Then Thinking

Professor Peter Gollwitzer of New York University says that many people who want to put their efforts into achieving great things, but don't, are derailed by seemingly small problems like these:

» They want to finish a task to a high standard, but a phone call disrupts them.

» They want to complete a coursework piece, but the weekend is just too busy.

» They want to do some serious revision, but some friends disturb them and the work is abandoned.

In their book *The Psychology of Action* (1996), Peter Gollwitzer and John Bargh argue that if this happens to you, it's because you have low 'implementation intention' – you *sort of* want to put in the effort, but you will be easily put off if one thing goes wrong.

The solution? Successful students anticipate these problems and plan for how they will respond to them with maximum effort. You sequence actions that anticipate obstacles and build-in pre-prepared solutions – you effectively beat self-sabotage before it even happens.

Consider these examples:

Student 1: 'I'll get started on this first thing in the morning.' This is a really common internal dialogue you might experience as a student – lots do it! And with one small disruption the whole plan comes to a standstill.

Student 2: 'I'll get started on this first thing in the morning. And …

» *If* I wake up late by accident, *then* I'll use my morning break to start it instead and …'

» *If* I feel really demotivated, *then* I'll get two coffees from the canteen and drink them quickly to give me a boost and …'

» *If* I get disturbed by friends, *then* I'll make an excuse and go to the library and …'

» *If* the internet is down, *then* I'll start by using my class notes and save the research work until later.'

It's easy to see which student might be the one most likely to succeed. Student 2 has listed a series of potential problems and has recognised their tendency to self-sabotage when small things go wrong. By planning a change in action when those small obstacles come along, they are much more likely to keep pushing forward.

List all the usual blockers you use to prevent high levels of effort and for each one commit to a solution. Think them all through in your head and make notes. What you are doing is strengthening your implementation intention. You *will* put the effort in, even if small things crop up to stop you.

Try it for a week!

3. Systems

As educators, we have consistently placed a high value on organisation skills. We have aspired to it ourselves and we have expected it from our students. However, we haven't offered any guidance on how to achieve this skill.

Garber (1983), p. 217

What Is A System?

A levels cover a lot of ground. Lessons typically take place in one-hour chunks, so A levels get taught in bits. Usually there are something like 130 lessons in a Year 12 curriculum and another 130 in Year 13. That's 260 bits to organise for each course. Most students do three A levels so, in total, that's 780 separate bits. If students can't organise these bits, they can't learn them. Our conversations with students show there is a direct link between their level of organisation and the final grade.

Students who jam their 780 bits of information randomly into a bag can put off disaster for a while, but eventually the exams will find them out. The better they are at organising the 780 bits of information, the better their final grade will be. Why? Because once they've organised all these bits, they can begin to see patterns, create connections and make sense of all the information. They can begin to really own it, recast it and master it at a deeper level. Students need a system that helps them do this.

When we say 'systems', we mean two things: (1) a system to organise learning so students can make sense of it all, and (2) a system to organise their time so students can complete key tasks to deadlines. We find this definition of systems much more helpful than the nebulous term 'study skills', which is tricky to define and serves to make the whole process seem more complex than it is.

If you model and teach project management skills, you will discover that students find it easier to focus on the cognitive aspects of their studies, they will suffer from less anxiety and stress, and they are more likely to be prepared when it comes to revision. They will also lead much less cluttered lives, sleep easier and be happier with their studies.

> There is a direct link between the level of a student's organisation and their final grade.

Project Management

Project management is the activity of planning and organising yourself and the resources you have in order to achieve long-term goals. The basic principles of project management aren't difficult and can be easily taught. You might not have thought about it like this, but A levels are like planning four (or maybe more) projects.

For students to be able to manage their time effectively they need to be able to prioritise

their work, determine the time that needs to be allocated to these priorities and then schedule the work. They might never have done anything like this before. Many of us hadn't at that age either; we've acquired a very specific set of systems and ways of working through university and in the world of work. It's often hard to think your way back to the days where you operated without them.

Collecting and Capturing

We think how you collect and capture information is key to A level success. It provides students with a useful record of their work, which is crucial when it comes to revision and assists with understanding. In addition, it helps students to improve their writing and analysis skills as they develop their notes. Finally, we believe that good note taking helps to make learning stick.

How do your students collect their notes? Are they thrown in a bag, or do they have them neatly organised? Do you do regular file checks? How do you support students who haven't yet developed these skills? Crucially, do students keep a record of the tasks they are required to do, and the deadlines for those tasks?

Bear in mind that many students might not have needed to rely on these records before now. During Key Stage 3 and 4, teachers and tutors might have been giving learners constant reminders. Friends will also be reminding each other of the homework coming up. This means that tasks which may have been entirely forgotten can be quickly recalled through constant contact with peers. Work can be readily copied or completed during morning break or on the bus into school. Parents might be another constant reminder of what needs doing.

The networks of teachers, tutors and peers in a school operate almost like an external hard drive which can store huge amounts of data – information about what needs to be done, when by, to what standard and so on – and students might well have grown used to this. At A level, however, young learners find they are no longer unified in large groups because they're all taking different subjects. Tasks are much more complex, coursework portfolios are specific to individuals, personal projects aren't transferable and copying on the bus just doesn't cut it anymore.

They need new systems, and it's up to us to supply them.

Reflecting

When students are running four or five projects at once (such as A level work, applying to university, a part-time job and an extended project qualification) it can often feel like everything is spinning out of control. Students need time to pause and reflect; some quiet time just to think and get organised.

We've found that successful students already do this naturally, but it's a habit that needs to be encouraged with many. Some of the activities that follow are designed to do this. It's worth sacrificing half an hour's delivery of content in return for neat folders, connected information and calmer students who feel they're more in control. Being organised is one of the most important skills any student can have.

Teacher Guidance for Systems Activities

17. The Energy Line

This is a prioritisation tool that allows students to place a series of tasks on a line, assessing them in terms of their urgency. Students get to empty their heads of everything they have to do in a set period – a fortnight works well for us.

This is one of our favourite systems activities and has been adapted from Scott Belsky's great book, *Making Ideas Happen* (2011). It has rescued a number of students who felt like they were in meltdown. It's far more effective than a to-do list and encourages some prioritisation. The activity works best if you create an A3 version of the Energy Line. You also need some small sticky notes.

First, get the student to empty their head of all the tasks they've got to complete. The metaphor of the external hard drive is a useful one here – you're encouraging students to store everything they need to be doing in one place. When they're emptying their heads, it's almost like detoxing. They're clearing out all those half-remembered tasks, nagging thoughts and doubts, vague recollections and worries. Encourage them to keep going for as long as they can. It can sometimes be useful to include both college related and personal tasks, particularly if they lead busy lives. Reassure them they will sleep better once they do this. They won't be plagued by sudden cold sweats at 3 in the morning as they remember a half-forgotten or missed deadline. This task is going to seriously improve the quality of their lives!

When they've completed the empty-their-head phase, start adding the sticky notes to the Energy Line. We've added a slight twist here: we only allow students to put two sticky notes in the extreme column, four in high, six in medium and then the rest have to be spread across low or idle. Why does this work? Students understandably feel like *all* their tasks are urgent. They can only work on one task at a time, so the Energy Line helps them focus on where to start. As they complete the task they can remove the sticky note from the Energy Line and move another up.

Make sure you check their prioritisation with them. When we first used this tool we assumed students could place tasks accurately. But prioritising can be clouded by emotions – tasks they dread might go in 'idle' for the wrong reasons. We've also seen students prioritise tasks because they are frightened of angering their teachers, not because the job needs doing urgently. A coaching discussion might be needed as the notes are positioned.

If you want to go deeper with this activity, you can get students to add the deadline date and the estimated time needed to complete the task to each note. Or lighten their load by asking them to do one task now – whichever one might take fifteen minutes or less – and pull it off the line.

18. The Breakfast Club

This activity asks students to consider their morning routine – the time of day when they should be at their peak – and what they do with that time. After answering a series of questions and discussing their morning routines, and the morning routines of others, students can then reschedule difficult tasks for morning study periods and make a commitment to tackling their most challenging work when they're at their freshest.

This gives students time and space to assess what their current patterns of

Students understandably feel like *all* their tasks are urgent.

behaviour are like, and also an opportunity to arrange their tasks in order of challenge so they can schedule them appropriately. As a coaching activity with an individual this works well, although you will need to give learners some time to prepare so the conversation is purposeful. It's successful with small groups too.

19. Snack, Don't Binge (or the Weekly Review)

This consists of a set of instructions for a reflective planning session which has been adapted from Dave Allen's *Getting Things Done* (2002). It creates a framework so students can spend an hour or so assessing exactly where they are up to with all the projects they're running.

We know that many students claim cramming works, but research shows that frequently reviewing work improves understanding and retention (Donovan and Radosevich, 1999). After completing a lesson, some students will never return to the crime scene until it's time for revision (or cramming).

The Weekly Review works well for students who adopt this mindset by encouraging them to constantly review their progress and reinforce their understanding. It can be used in one-to-one coaching sessions or as a group activity. We've worked with sixth forms where curriculum areas have built this into

their schemes of work, so that every fortnight or so students are given twenty or thirty minutes to consider their learning, sequence their tasks, look at areas of weakness and ask their teacher for advice. It can take as little as ten or fifteen minutes at the end or beginning of a week to review the previous week's work.

Of course, you will get subject teachers – even students! – telling you in no uncertain terms that they haven't got time to stop and do this type of activity. We disagree, but even so, once it's been modelled a couple of times, you might just as well set it as a weekly homework task.

20. The 2–4–8 Rule

This is a simple planning activity for students which involves dissecting a long-term project and breaking it down into a number of smaller sub-deadlines. It's helpful for both short- and long-term projects. It provides the students with some milestones to aim for and helps them chunk down larger tasks.

We've found it useful to get students to draw a bridge on A4 paper, so that they can visualise how project management is like building a bridge across a valley or chasm. This imaginary bridge spans a large, open valley, so they will need vertical piers supporting it as it crosses the space. These become the 'delivery points' in time. In these vertical supports, students can list the milestones they would like to achieve by each specific point. As they cross from the present (i.e. where they are) to the future (i.e. where they want to be), they have to ensure they are delivering at each mini-deadline.

21–23. STQR/ Project Progress Chart/ The Eisenhower Matrix

Like the Energy Line, these are helpful visual tools which students can use to categorise and assess a whole list of jobs. Swap between them – each might have a slightly different effect on the students, and often the appeal of these systems is very personal. We've grouped these three tools together because we often introduce them all at the same time to a whole year group, and then give the students some time to play around with them and decide which ones work best for them.

These three tools also work on assessing the progress of big projects, such as completing a piece of coursework, revising the entire content of a course or even assessing progress in all four courses at once. The grids are all effective ways of breaking down and re-prioritising. We print the grids on A3 or A4 paper so the students can write in the boxes. This can then be stuck on their wall at home to remind them of the timescale of the project ahead.

24. The Lead Domino

This is a neat prioritisation tool – and an unusual one – which works well particularly for students with attention management issues. The learner lists all the jobs and tasks they have to do, or have recently completed, and then makes an assessment of how effective and efficient their prioritisation has been. They audit how they currently spend their time and then make an assessment of whether that time has been spent effectively. Essentially, you are looking to throw some light on unnecessary tasks the student may be completing and explore task avoidance.

The way to frame it is like this. We've all got a limited supply of effort – something that applies particularly when we're in the early stages of developing and strengthening positive habit loops. New habits can tire us out in the early stages. One metaphor we're fond of using when explaining this is the notion of 'effort points'. You begin the day with a certain number: early on in A level study you might only have twelve effort points to spend per day, and when they're gone you're totally wiped out and exhausted. As you get stronger and more determined you might have twenty points per day. Or fifty.

So, given that your effort stock is finite – and your list requires more points than you've got to spend – what are the best jobs to get done? The Lead Domino is the answer – the ugly job, the uncomfortable one, the one after which everything else looks easy. If you can, get a commitment from the student during your discussion to finish it by the end of the day. Then issue a reward – something small like a verbal pat on the back, a coffee or a chocolate bar. Knowing how to choose the Lead Domino is a habit they will thank you for one day.

We've found this works best as a one-to-one coaching tool as there is usually quite a bit of questioning required to get the student to a point where they identify the Lead Domino and agree that this is where they should be putting their time and effort. It can be uncomfortable – inevitably, students try to minimise the importance of tasks they don't want to do, and sometimes you have to be the one to tell them to tackle the job that they are subconsciously avoiding.

17. Systems Activity: The Energy Line

Many students feel overwhelmed by the amount of work they have to do. Some keep lists – scribbling down jobs and crossing them off when they're done. And lists are good – they help you keep on top of what it is you've got to do.

The drawback of a list is that it doesn't tell you what to do first. A better tool to use for prioritising tasks is an Energy Line – it beats a to-do list any day of the week. It helps you put things in order according to how much effort you need to give them. Put things on the left-hand side – high or extreme – if you need to work like mad on them. Put them on the right if you can kick back and leave it for a bit. Attach dates for submission and you're really getting there. Write the jobs on sticky notes and move them around, taking them off altogether when they're done. Scott Belsky suggests this technique in his book *Making Ideas Happen* (2011). We love it!

Organising

Try prioritising actions on an Energy Line.

How much are you going to put into getting them done?

Some will need a big energy push – you'll need to be working at them every day.

Others will tick over – you'll need to work at them once a week.

Extreme	High	Medium	Low	Idle

18. Systems Activity: The Breakfast Club

In *Sex Sleep Eat Drink Dream: A Day in the Life of Your Body*, Jennifer Ackerman (2008) shares some research which suggests that for most people, the brain is at its sharpest in the first four hours after waking. Not straightaway – it needs time to get up to speed. But then it hits a sweet spot when it's really firing. Brain efficiency can vary, she says, but in the morning it can be up to 30% more active and sharp than it is at other times.

Here's something else to consider: the longer the day goes on, the more self-control problems you will have. If you're trying to give up chocolate, for example, you will rarely crack at 10 a.m. But by 4.30 p.m., when you're feeling tired, your self-control slips. It's the same with work. If you tell yourself you will start a big project at 3 p.m. or 6 p.m., the chances of that happening are low. If you set aside some 'breakfast club' time – sweet spot time in the morning – you're much more likely to clear the job.

And yet we often see students using a morning study period to ease themselves into the day. They waste their moments of high brain energy on social media and gaming, then turn their attention to work later on when they're not as productive.

The Morning Routine

With all this in mind, look at your morning routine. Make some notes under the following headings:

» What time do you wake up?

» What do you do with your first hour?

» What are your habits and rituals, your repeated behaviours?

» Are they positive? Do they set you up for a good day?

» How long do they take? Are they worth it?

Scheduling

Now look at the work you have to do this week. Use the Energy Line to figure out what's coming up in terms of deadlines, then:

» Take your highest priority tasks (or your hardest or trickiest tasks) and schedule them in morning slots for the whole week.

» Commit to clearing them early in the day. Stick with it, and at the end of the period discuss what went well and what needs adjusting as a result.

19. Systems Activity: Snack, Don't Binge (or the Weekly Review)

Studies show that cramming or bingeing on learning isn't as successful as snacking on it. In other words, students do significantly better if they review their learning regularly rather than if they leave it to pile up, and then try to deal with it all at once. Your productivity – the amount of efficient and effective work you do – is significantly improved by doing the work frequently.

Here's a habit to work on developing. It's called the Weekly Review. Follow these steps and you will find yourself snacking – checking your learning regularly – instead of bingeing!

1 Set aside an hour a week. This time must be sacred – don't let anyone disturb you! Put your phone on aeroplane mode, go offline and never swap your hour for something else or skip it. Make it a crucial part of your week. We suggest a Friday afternoon or a Monday morning.

2 Split up the hour evenly. We suggest fifteen minutes per course. Be strict with yourself.

3 For fifteen minutes, review the week's work in that course. We suggest the following:

» Check your notes are clear, legible and in order.

» Summarise your learning in a quick diagram, mind-map or a few lines of notes.

» Highlight or circle material you've found hard this week. This is the stuff you will need to work on during your independent study time.

» Go through the jobs you've been given and the deadlines you've got. Make a prioritised list for the week ahead.

4 Once you've done this four times, once for each subject, you should be feeling pretty good. You're in control. You know what needs to be done.

Students who make a habit of the Weekly Review are often much calmer and less stressed. They can leave school on Friday knowing they're on top of things. They've emptied their heads of all the little niggling worries that might keep them awake at night.

Students who make a habit of the Weekly Review are often much calmer and less stressed.

20. Systems Activity: The 2–4–8 Rule

This is a simple system of time management. It's based on the idea of a long-term project being like a bridge. Imagine a bridge built over a wide valley. What kind of bridge are you imagining? We would bet it has vertical piers holding it up. That's because everyone knows that something which spans a long distance needs regular structure to support it.

Now imagine that bridge as a long-term project – an essay that needs to be handed in to your teacher in two weeks or a coursework project that needs to be submitted in three months. The project is a long-term, long-distance project, so it needs a regular structure to support it. The 2–4–8 rule helps you build that solid structure, like vertical piers supporting a bridge.

1. The Short-Term Project: 'You've got two weeks to complete this'

Many teachers might give you two weeks to complete a project. Here's how to use the 2–4–8 rule to respond:

» **Target 1:** two days. Make a note of what you would like to achieve to get the project started – a side of writing, three hours of reading, some research, organising your notes or planning your piece. Set yourself a target of two days to complete this work.

» **Target 2:** four days later. Make a note of where you want to be four days after that. Halfway through would be a sensible plan. Break the back of the task – get through the hard bit.

» **Target 3:** eight days later. You're handing in the assignment today. It needs to be complete. Make sure you've finished early, gone through it and made any adjustments.

2. The Long-Term Project: 'This needs finishing by March'

Often coursework submissions come with more extended deadlines like this. If your deadline is a longer one, it's worth working backwards from targets like this:

» **Target 3:** eight months until submission. In these early stages, you should be finding an example of what you're trying to achieve – for example, another student's coursework submission. Look it over and say to yourself, 'I want mine to look like this.' Make a list of what needs to be done by the end of the project. Get started on rough, early versions or drafts.

» **Target 2:** four months until submission. Make notes of where you would like to be halfway through, assuming it's going really well. By now you will have been working on early versions and fleshing them out. How many sections will be complete in rough form by this point? What will your word count be (if it's a written task)? What reading and research will you have done and incorporated by this point? What standard will you have achieved?

» **Target 1:** two months until submission. If you've met your targets up until this point, you'll know very clearly what needs to be done to complete the project, and you can begin the final stages in earnest. What groundwork do you still need to do? What reading needs to be completed? What notes do you still need to take and incorporate? How many words are left to write? How do you conclude and reference your work?

21. Systems Activity: STQR

Successful project managers suggest you begin any huge project (like passing an A level) with an understanding of the following four things:

SCOPE The size of the project

TIME Completion by when?

QUALITY The standards you want

RESOURCE Staff, students, VLE, library, exam papers ...

The first is scope – the size of the project. This is crucial: how big is the job ahead of you? Surprisingly, lots of students never really get to grips with what they need to know.

Second is the time frame. You need to consider two things here: when is the deadline for the project, and how many hours will you need to complete it? Thinking in terms of hours will give you a much clearer idea when it comes to scheduling the project.

Third is quality. Not only do you have to consider the standards you want to achieve, but you also need to know the criteria you are working towards. What exactly do you have to do to meet the standards? Write these down in this box.

Finally, in the resources box list everything you will need to complete the project. This can also include people – for example, you might have to meet certain teachers.

22. Systems Activity: Project Progress Chart

This is a simple tool to keep track of where you are with everything on which you're working. Whether you're taking three or four A level courses, applying to university, taking general studies, organising some work shadowing or completing an extended project qualification, the number of projects you're running at one time can sometimes be a bit overwhelming.

The Project Progress Chart helps you track where you are with each one. List every job or task you've got to do and place them somewhere on the grid. It will help you prioritise what to do next.

On the horizontal axis is *time*. Projects ahead of schedule go far right and projects lagging behind go far left. On the vertical axis is *quality*. Projects heading for a high quality finish go at the top and projects that are running on a low quality go towards the bottom.

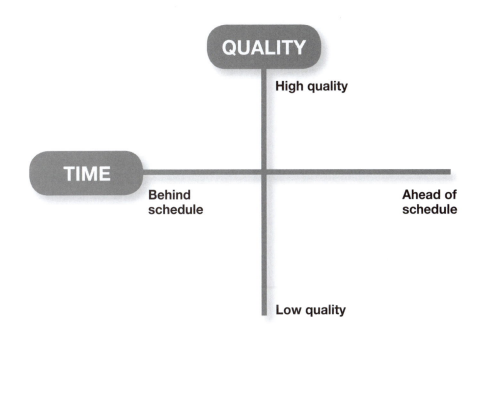

23. Systems Activity: The Eisenhower Matrix

This model was supposedly developed by US President Dwight Eisenhower – he was considered a master of time management, always getting everything done by the deadline. His famous alleged quote, 'I have two kinds of problems, the urgent and the important. The urgent are not important, and the important are never urgent,' led to the development of what is now referred to as the Eisenhower Matrix, which is used all over the world in business.

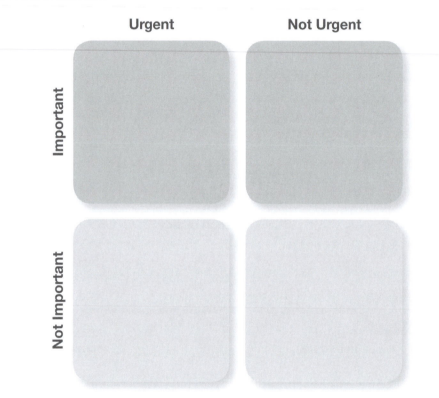

Eisenhower put all his tasks into one of four boxes on the matrix. He then dealt with the ones that were urgent and important. Only when all the tasks in this box were complete did he move on to the other boxes.

Now try to organise your tasks using this framework!

24. Systems Activity: The Lead Domino

What Should I Focus My Time On?

Tim Ferriss, an entrepreneur and business adviser who is behind www.fourhourworkweek.com, recommends two tactics for helping you to decide where to focus your time to get maximum gains. He argues that a lot of work can be saved by focusing on jobs that will have the biggest knock-on effects.

These are the two principles he recommends when choosing your next task.

Go for the 'Lead Domino'

In his podcast, 'How to Build a Large Audience from Scratch (and More)', Ferriss argues that you should put your effort into the one job which, when done, will render the largest number of other jobs either easier or irrelevant. In other words, the job that has the largest number of positive knock-on effects.

When you've got a list of things to do, use this principle to guide where you put your effort. It will stop you (as Professor Randy Pausch puts it) 'polishing the underside of the banister' – in other words, spending time doing jobs that aren't necessary (see Frogs and Banisters on page 49 for extra advice on this one).

Go for the Task Which Makes You Feel Most Uncomfortable

With this second piece of advice, Ferriss makes the point that, subconsciously, we often know which are the big, important jobs because they make us feel challenged or uncomfortable. There is a significant crossover between tasks that make us feel uncomfortable and tasks that are going to be important and improve us quickly.

The job that makes you feel anxious is likely to be your Lead Domino. And by focusing on it now, you will save time and effort later.

4. Practice

Practice should not be a punishment. When you invest the time and creativity to make practice fun, people will be motivated to participate, not only out of sheer enjoyment but also because you are communicating an important message: this is something positive that is worth our time. Lemov (2012), p. 156

What Is Practice?

We see practice as distinct from effort; it represents what learners do with the time they put into their studies. Not the *how much* of study but the *how*. It was the last element of the VESPA model to arrive and it remained stubbornly out of reach for a couple of years. We had been experiencing some interesting conundrums with students who were working hard – every effort questionnaire and intervention activity told us they were putting in the hours – but they weren't making the progress we expected of them.

Fixed mindset students in this situation were giving us the fixed mindset story – 'I'm really trying, but I just haven't got what it takes.' Fixed mindset staff were telling us the same thing – 'I'm afraid this learner is willing but just too weak to succeed.' We knew this wasn't true, although for some time we couldn't suggest a robust alternative. That was until we decided to speak to these students and closely analyse what it was they were doing with all this time they were putting in to their studies. The results were at once startling and obvious.

Tom Stafford and Michael Dewar (2014) found that when it comes to learning quickly, it's the way you practice not how often you practice that counts. They analysed data from 854,064 players on an online game looking at how practice affected subsequent performances. Practice doesn't make perfect. Perfect practice makes perfect. In other words, effort alone is not enough to guarantee success. Academic progress is as much about how you work as it is about how long you work for. The students who were putting in large amounts of time and effort, but not making progress, were working on the wrong things.

So what are the right things? We tried to categorise and subdivide the process of learning and mastery. Here's what we came up with:

1 **Content.** The learner masters the content taught by reviewing and consolidating it, checking it and ensuring understanding.

2 **Skills.** The learner puts this knowledge into practice in high stakes contexts; they practise exam questions, time themselves, try tough questions and complete mock tests.

3 **Feedback.** The learner seeks out expert feedback that allows them to develop their performance.

Deep learning requires a good distribution of time and effort across all three elements of the process.

When we spoke to high-effort-low-progress students, and asked them to check off every learning activity they completed regularly on a huge list, it emerged that they only completed step 1. They stayed where they were most comfortable – they reviewed content. They had upped the effort level – they might be spending many hours at it – but they hadn't broadened the scope of their practice. And why should they? Exams at Key Stage 4, for many of our young learners, require understanding of a specific amount of content. It's entirely logical that students taking A levels might assume the same. And even if they have realised that the courses are harder, long established learning habits are hard to break. Some of the students we spoke to almost hated themselves for it: 'I know I shouldn't be doing this – but I just sort of have to …'

There are a number of signs that this is happening. Watch out for learners who spend hours with intricately designed flash cards, learners who feel compelled to copy all their notes out again before they can begin learning them, students who endlessly re-read textbooks or those who look for new and different ways to review content even when they've mastered it (e.g. watching videos which recap familiar material). The clincher? Anyone who claims, 'You can't really revise for this subject', by which they mean: this subject demands skill development – I only know how to review content.

Know the Skills

One problem for learners fixated on constantly reviewing content is they might not know the skills associated with step 2 (i.e. what the exam requires of them).

First, and most obviously, they need to know the exam well. They need a huge number of exam papers to roam through, experiment with and explore. Supply students with these. Make them up if you have to. Don't expect reluctant or frightened learners to seek them out by providing a hyperlink or web address and then despairing when they don't visit. High stakes practice is uncomfortable; any normal person will avoid it.

Second, generate skills lists. We've done this with a whole range of A levels. Success at any A level subject is the result of mastering six, seven or maybe eight skills. Check assessment objectives for ideas. Staff might naturally cite content – 'Students need to know about …' – but that's step 1 stuff. The question you need to ask is, 'I'm not interested in what they need to *know*. I'm interested in what they need to be able to *do*.' Keep seeking it out, honing and simplifying, and you will end up with a skills checklist. With a list of skills that will ensure success, students can begin practising in earnest.

Practice Under a Variety of Conditions

Joshua Foer (2012, p. 173) argues that 'if they're not practicing deliberately, even experts can see their skills backslide'. A drill is a specifically designed task that very deliberately strengthens a learner's skill in a particular area. Once you know what skills you're trying to develop, you can design drills to develop those skills. Drills commonly take away the time constraints of 'game conditions' to allow slow and deliberate focus.

We've found the following distinction between mechanical practice and flexible practice helpful when designing drills and encouraging effective practice.

Mechanical practice repeats a very similar activity over and over again. It works for rigid, unvarying tasks that challenge learners at the base of Bloom's taxonomy. It should not account for all student practice. Too much reliance on mechanical practice leads to exam meltdown when questions are even slightly unfamiliar. 'It threw me!' students will understandably say. 'I just panicked!'

Flexible practice is less predictable. Unusual factors such as unexpected variables or elements are introduced to the practice. Here's a simple way of doing it: use a high level question from a different syllabus and ask, 'What would you do if you saw this question?' Students need to expect the unexpected and be psychologically ready for it, particularly as linear syllabuses and exams begin throwing in curveballs to differentiate the top learners.

The Example-Rich Environment

The final principle to bear in mind: A levels aren't rocket science. Demystify them. Don't allow students to believe the 'you've either got it or you haven't' narrative. Don't give the impression that there is 'guild knowledge' – that is, mysterious information or processes only clever people understand or need to know. Don't tell students their answer is 'missing flair' or 'lacks a special something'.

Instead, use a simple and clear approach. Something like this: 'Your work is grade B at the moment because it displays these characteristics … Here's a grade A piece. Can you see the difference? Let's analyse the A grade example together and figure out how to close the gap.'

A very straightforward way of expressing this is through the 'more of, less of' model. Here, you specify two behaviours typical of a student's work, one positive and one negative. Then, having looked at an example, you can encourage the student to do more of one thing and less of another. Then ask them to try it again.

Needless to say, learners will make the quickest progress if they are given an example of a skill executed at A, B, C, D and E grade, so they can explore and understand the differences between them.

> **A drill is a specifically designed task that strengthens a learner's skill in a particular area. Once you know what skills you're trying to develop, you can design drills to develop those skills.**

Teacher Guidance for Practice Activities

25. The Revision Questionnaire

This is another one of our questionnaires, although this is one that needs to be properly conducted and analysed. It is the starting point for any analysis of practice – you can deliver it to an individual, a small group or a full class. We've had success presenting it to a hall full of 200 students, who all filled it in quietly. We then gathered in the forms and talked them through the stages of revision and practice. The questionnaires were sorted by tutor group and examined later; students got feedback about where they were spending their practice time and how they could adjust to maximise performance. Students can do a simple 'I must do more of …' and 'I must do less of …' analysis once they've reflected on their current practice. You can challenge them to add a revision method every week and reflect on its impact. Try redistributing the questionnaires after a period of learning – half-termly reminders of how to practice can be a good way to start Year 12.

If you want to take it large scale (and we recommend that you do) you can audit the behaviours of a whole year group or, as we did, the Year 12 cohort across three schools to make sure our institution was broadly in line with the others (it was). We put the questionnaire online and got groups of students in IT suites to complete it. The key here, we reckon, is mixing up the revision methods so they don't sit neatly in the three stages (i.e. content work, skills and feedback) as they do in the version here. That way, you can be sure each method is taken at face value and all are considered and assessed equally. It's not a statistically watertight questionnaire – we know that. But it gives you a chance to break down the percentage of time your students are spending, on average, on each stage of revision.

It's worth trying this simple thought experiment. If the whole of your cohort filled in this questionnaire and the results were analysed, what proportion of their time would the students be spending on content work, skills work and feedback work? Ponder it and come up with your three figures. Ours are tucked away at the bottom of the page.*

26. Know the Skills

The students are presented with a diagram – it looks a little like a pie chart – that allows them to audit their skill development in a particular subject. They identify the things they need to be able to do well in order to succeed, assign a slice of 'pie' to each skill and then self-assess by colouring in a certain proportion of each slice. It provides a good visual representation of their current performance and a clear picture for where they need to focus their practice.

It works superbly, on one condition: your teachers can explain to the students the six or seven skills necessary for mastery of their A level subject. Back when we developed this tool, we could do it for our own subjects with little bother.

Here's an example from A level English literature, in which (at the time of writing) you need to be able to:

1 Structure and organise an argument.

2 Choose appropriate quotes from the text to support it.

* We're rounding up for simplicity's sake. When we first did this, 80% of student time was spent revising content, 15% was spent developing skills and a depressing 5% was spent seeking specific and actionable feedback with experts. The first step to changing this is surfacing it.

3 Comment on a writer's use of form, structure and language.

4 Understand and acknowledge the different critical perspectives from which a text can be assessed.

5 Comment confidently on the socio-historical context of the text.

6 Make purposeful and illuminating connections between texts you are comparing.

7 Communicate effectively using appropriate terminology.

That's it. No guild knowledge. No special flair or knack. Once you have identified the key six or seven skills, you can confidently tell your class, 'You can all get a grade A. What you need to master are the following seven skills … Let's start practising them.'

The trouble with this activity comes when teachers struggle to name the skills required for success. They might keep returning to content when you ask them. You might get, 'They need to know all about …' No. That's content, not skills. You're not after what they need to know; you're after what they need to do with what they know. So when a teacher says, 'They really need to understand …', stop them and ask them to rephrase: 'Assuming they understand it, what do they need to be able to *do*?'

We're all too focused on content sometimes, but for the sake of these activities let's assume that the students do understand the content. Let's not flatter ourselves – it's not that difficult to grasp the content of most A level courses. Assume they will get it and we're free to shift our focus to skill development.

One thing to watch out for: be wary if a subject leader tells you there are twenty or thirty skills necessary for mastery of their subject. We spent a long time unpicking this one. When we dug deeper they were almost always listing content. Instead, start with the assessment objectives – always a good place for a list of skills rather than knowledge.

Once you've got that straight you can audit skill development – and this activity works a treat. We find it useful with subject-specific groups who know the skills they're trying to develop. The visual audit helps to guide their revision and preparation.

27. Graphic Organisers

Students need to own their knowledge. That means recasting it in some way – putting it into their own words, into shapes and pictures, and securing it in their own thoughts. Graphic organisers help learners to recast information. In this activity, we suggest a whole bunch of different graphic organisers that might help them and give them time to play with each one. Tables, charts, diagrams and metaphors are all used, and each in their own way forces students to reshape information in a way that helps them master it.

It's important that we push students away from the atomistic (i.e. secure knowledge of a small syllabus area divorced from the remaining learning) to the holistic (i.e. complete and connected understanding). We use a couple of diagrams to illustrate this on the activity sheet – these are worth exploring with the student. At all times you're asking, 'How do things connect?' Graphic organisers help learners to make these strides forward. You can encourage a whole group of students to do this together. Group work can really accelerate progress when you use some of the more complex organisers, particularly in mixed ability groups.

The suggestions for the different graphic organisers are differentiated. Students new to a topic could try a mind-map or comparison table – both are organisers which clarify and consolidate learning without significantly recasting it. Push students towards metaphors (e.g. the tree, the village, the river) as these encourage them to classify learning more creatively, and this pushes them towards connections they might not have seen before. Share good examples!

28. The Leitner Box

The Leitner Box is an organisational system which uses a series of flash cards. The students will need the flash cards first, so this is an activity that comes into play for us early in the revision season. The session encourages them to sort their flash cards in new and innovative ways to encourage more focused and purposeful practice.

This is a session that we've found works brilliantly with students who have become wedded to flash cards, gel pens and highlighters, who have a religious devotion to content learning at the expense of skills and feedback. We use this predominantly with individuals – you will see why when you look it over. By categorising their flash cards, you're requiring students to self-assess their current level of understanding, which makes them more critical. Then you're forcing them out of the comfortable relearning of familiar information and into a much more challenging place.

One thing that's worth a mention here – a very wise and effective member of our sixth form team is fond of pointing this out to students: flash cards and notes are simply a record of learning. They, in themselves, are not revision. Any student who, at the end of a course, begins the process of assembling a set of killer course notes on flash cards – a process which takes them, say, the full month before the day of the exam – is kidding themselves. That work should have been done as they went along. Revision and practice is about mastery of content and skills, not a laborious rewriting of it all. The notes and cards should be created as you learn the material, not at the end. Simple but true.

29. Two Slow, One Fast

This is a skills development drill which requires students to repeat a tricky process three times. It must be a process specific to one of their courses – for example, a complex calculation, a paragraph from an essay or a short response to an exam question. You will need to block out some time for them to do this.

We once demonstrated this to a history teacher at another organisation, and a few weeks later she came back to us, delighted with the results. We've found that it works well with subjects that require extended writing or mathematical problem solving. It's a good coaching tool too – we tend to use it one to one.

Don't forget that students find it borderline painful to go so slowly. Often you will get a rebuke along the lines of, 'We have thirty minutes to do this in the exam! Why are we spending an hour on it?' Explain that the fast bit comes later. Nail the slow bit first. This encourages a mindful, reflective attention to the task. For further information on how going slow builds skill, check out Dan Coyle's wonderful book, *The Talent Code* (2009), and read about how musicians and tennis players use this technique.

30. Right, Wrong, Right

This is a variation on the previous drill, again requiring students to repeat a task three times. On this occasion, though, they need to see a model of the skill (e.g. a calculation, a paragraph, a short answer) executed more successfully than they are currently capable of themselves. This is great for taking a C grade performance up to a B grade, for example, and works best with a single student or a small group who are making similar errors. We adapted this from Dan Coyle's sandwich technique in *The Little Book of Talent* (2012).

A couple of years ago, one of our brightest and best students gave us some feedback, the way students do by way of thanks at the end of their Year 13 courses. His comment went something like this (apologies if we mangle it – you know who you are!): 'You've suggested some really crazy stuff this year. But the best thing you ever did was show me that right, wrong, right thing.' (He was right about the crazy stuff. That year we had done a session where we made students 'power pose' before challenging tests and exams. It worked! Check out Amy Cuddy and colleagues' (2012) research if you want to know more.)

31. Learning from Mistakes

In this activity students audit the feedback they've been getting from teachers. They will need their files with them and a series of marked pieces of work from particular subjects. They use a grid to record feedback, with their attention firmly fixed on the types of errors they've made. We encourage learners to categorise their errors and give them three places to start: active mistakes, where the wrong process is chosen for the task; slip-ups, where the correct process is chosen but there is a problem with execution; and blackouts, where the student doesn't know the content well enough. By reflecting on the kinds of errors they're making, students can adjust their practice to compensate.

Here's how we've got the best out of it. Talk the students through James Reason's research in *A Life in Error* (2013) and ask them to critically assess his categorisations of errors. We've found that some groups – depending on the subjects they take – pretty much accept his definitions and go with them. Others aren't so sure and instead draw up a list of other possible errors. This works well if students pick through examples of D or E grade work, creating a hit-list of errors to avoid. It's a decent activity to do in teams or groups, and when you come together again you can redesign the grid with the new error types in them. Together, you can develop suggested solutions to those errors.

Finally, you can get students to audit their last three attempts at an exam question and finish with a 'more of, less of' analysis.

32. Mechanical vs. Flexible

This is a simple account of two types of practice – mechanical/repetitive practice and flexible/challenging practice – followed by some suggestions about how to develop flexibility. We developed this in response to students whose practice was very repetitive and rigid, because the key to accelerating learning quickly is practice that is interleaved, varied, unexpected and challenging.

This is a good discussion activity and can be followed up by students making a commitment to try more flexible practice. It's also a good activity to use with students who want to be top performers.

> **Don't expect reluctant or frightened learners to seek out exam papers by providing a hyperlink or web address and then despairing when they don't visit. High stakes practice is uncomfortable; any normal person will avoid it.**

25. Practice Activity: The Revision Questionnaire

We've found there is a strong link between the kind of revision someone does and the outcomes they get. So, which student will do better in an exam?

» Student 1 does fifteen hours' revision – all of it reading through class notes.

» Student 2 only does ten hours' revision – two hours making mind-maps, two hours creating flash cards of key terms, three hours writing timed essays, two hours working through past papers and looking for patterns in the questions asked, and half an hour doing the hardest question they could find, followed by half an hour talking it through with their teacher. Then they spend five hours shopping with their friends and watching TV.

You too can make less mean more. Try this questionnaire:

Name: _____   Subject: _____

1 How many hours of independent work do you do on your subjects outside of class? Please state the time spent on each subject.

2 What sort of activities do you do? Use the table below:

		Always	Sometimes	Never
Reading through class notes	C			
Using resources on the school's VLE	C			
Using course textbooks	C			
Mind-maps/diagrams	C			
Making/remaking class notes	C			
Highlighting/colour coding	C			
Flash cards	C			
Using a revision wall to display your learning	C			
Writing exam answers under timed conditions	S			
Reading model answers	S			

Using past exam questions and planning answers	S			
Marking your own work to a mark scheme	F			
Studying mark schemes or examiners' reports	F			
Working with other students in groups/pairs	F			
Comparing model answers against your own work	F			
Creating your own exam questions	F			
Handing in extra exam work for marking	F			
One-to-one discussions with teachers/tutors	F			

3 Additional activities not mentioned above:

4 Write a brief account of what you do if you can't understand something (e.g. try again, read textbooks, check the school's VLE, see teachers, see other students).

You will notice some activities have a 'C' next to them – these are the *content* techniques. Some activities have an 'S' next to them – these are the *skills* techniques. Others have an 'F' next to them – these are the *feedback* techniques.

Notice in our example that student 1 only does content revision, while student 2 does all three stages and then takes some time off. In our experience, student 2 will pretty much always get a better grade than student 1. And they put in fewer hours.

Make sure you do some revision for each of C, S and F!

Practice

26. Practice Activity: Know the Skills

It's almost impossible to practise the component skills of a subject if you don't know what those skills are. Once you do know, you can put them into a target diagram like the one below. Target diagrams like this are used by sports psychologists when working with athletes.

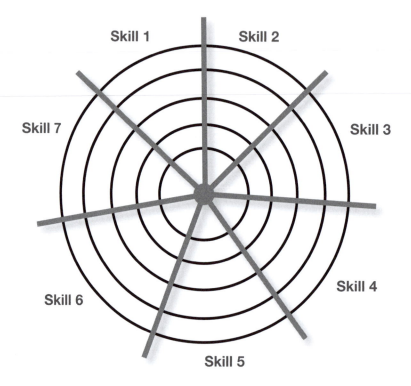

The slice of the target diagram is coloured in depending on how confident and practised you feel with a particular skill – a fully coloured in slice for a skill that you feel is fully developed and a totally empty slice for a skill that needs a lot of work.

Meet your teachers and ask them, 'What are the seven skills I need to master to get an A?' Read your syllabuses and look at the assessment objectives (AOs), which are the skills the examiner is looking for. Then begin a regular self-assessment of those skills.

'What are the seven skills I need to master to get an A?'

27. Practice Activity: Graphic Organisers

There is a difference between information and knowledge.

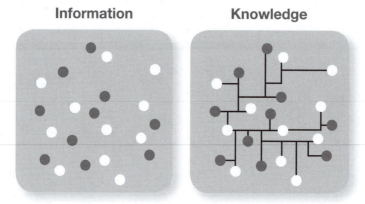

Information   **Knowledge**

Information, on the left, is a loose collection of facts, with no connections between them, no overall understanding, so there is very little we can do with it. Information won't help you pass an exam or master a skill. On the right, you can see that knowledge is connected information. The job of any learner is to turn information into knowledge.

So how do we build these connections to turn information into knowledge? One way is by reorganising pieces of information.

Graphic organisers can help you do this. Some are very simple:

» Make a mind-map of the information.

» Make a comparison table and pull out similarities and differences between two studies, methods, people, characters or historical events.

» Make a flow chart to summarise a process or series of events.

» Make a graph to represent the data.

Notice the focus on action here – each of our suggestions begins with 'make'. That's you being active, engaging with information and reorganising it so it becomes knowledge.

Alternatively you can use complex graphic organisers. They usually take the form of a metaphor, where you turn something into something else.

For example, summarise everything you know about a topic using the metaphor of a tree:

» What key information forms the trunk?

» What underlying information makes the roots?

» What are the important branches?

» What subsections of information become the twigs and leaves?

If this metaphor works for you, try the following:

» A castle with separate turrets and a strong foundation.

» A stream growing into a river and then a lake.

» A village with a central square and streets around it.

28. Practice Activity: The Leitner Box

The Leitner Box, which was developed by a German scientist called Sebastian Leitner, is a really effective, easy-to-develop practice and recall system. It's based on using flash cards to learn and then recall information, so this activity will need a whole bunch of subject-related flash cards. The cards are used as normal to record quick, easy-to-read bullet-pointed information about topics.

Leitner suggests that when we have a large amount of information to learn on flash cards, we have a tendency to gravitate towards the cards we already know and subconsciously avoid those we find difficult. To circumvent this, you create four subsections in your box (or four separate boxes):

» **Box 1.** Here you put items for frequent practice. This is the stuff you're not remembering well – it needs regular review and rereading because you're making mistakes when you practise recalling it or you don't know it at all. Around 40% of your time should be spent hammering the content of these cards. When you score a victory and fully recall a card, you move it down to box 2.

» **Box 2.** About 30% of your time is spent here. It's the stuff you've only just moved out of box 1 or learning that still trips you up or confuses you in any way. This material should be moving up (if you're not remembering it) or down (if you've nailed it) fairly regularly.

» **Box 3.** You spend 20% of your time here, and you nearly always get this stuff correct when you test yourself on it. You feel confident, even when the material is complex. However, if you dip in here and make any mistakes in recall at all, the card must be moved into box 2.

» **Box 4.** You begin with only a small number of cards here. This is the material you consider easy. You always get it right, so you only need to spend 10% of your time checking stuff in this box. However, and this is key, nothing ever leaves this box because you know it so well. No matter how confident you feel, you still check it every now and again.

If you practise your recall in this way, you will find you won't neglect information. You won't get caught by the 'familiarity trap' – the feeling that you know something so well you never need to test yourself on it. Plus, you keep your focus where it needs to be: on the tough stuff you keep forgetting.

29. Practice Activity: Two Slow, One Fast

This idea is borrowed from the sporting world. In sport, the word 'drill' is often used to describe practice. A drill is a specific and focused practice where all the chaos and uncertainty of the actual game is removed. Instead, a single skill is focused on and repeated. After some time working on a drill, players might then play a game in which the particular skill is tested.

Does this work with study too? With a maths problem or a history essay? The answer is yes.

» **Go slow.** To begin with you should try the equivalent of a drill. You're taking out the stress, worry and complexity, so you're not thinking about the chaos and uncertainty of doing an exam. You're going slowly, paying attention to what you do. That might mean taking half an hour to work through a short answer exam question, twenty minutes on a maths problem, an hour on a couple of science questions or half an hour writing a single killer paragraph for an essay.

» **Go fast.** Then you can try to apply the learning in a 'game' situation – in other words, under exam conditions. Pick an exam question, work out how long you would have in the exam and see whether you can perform at the same level but under the pressure of time.

Two Slow, One Fast describes the best sequence for developing a skill. Do it twice slowly and safely, paying attention to exactly what you're doing and why you're doing it. Then do it fast and see how you cope. You won't be perfect first time, but you will certainly accelerate the speed at which you get better.

The two rights start to burn the understanding into your brain. The wrong in the middle helps you see why the wrong is wrong.

30. Practice Activity: Right, Wrong, Right

One way to burn understanding into your brain, particularly a skill, is to find someone who does it well. It might be your teacher or a fellow student, someone in your class or someone in the year above. Find an example of them doing it right. It might be a complex mathematical problem worked through, a definition and example question in social science, a perfect paragraph or a calculation in chemistry or physics.

Once you've got the example, you can do the following activity. We've found it works well at helping students see the difference between a successful answer and unsuccessful answer by making you focus on the differences between wrong and right.

The principle is very simple. It goes like this:

1 Using your example, copy the skill. You must do it right. It might be that you write a paragraph that borrows the best bits from the example you've got, or you might solve a very similar mathematical problem following your example.

2 Then do it wrong. Do it the way you've been doing it. Examine the differences. Where exactly do you go wrong? What is the result of that error? Where does it lead? How does wrong look different?

3 Then copy the skill right again.

You go – right, wrong, right. The two rights start to burn the understanding into your brain. The wrong in the middle helps you see why the wrong is wrong.

31. Practice Activity: Learning from Mistakes

Professor James Reason of the University of Manchester has done a lot of work about mistakes that lead to disasters (aeroplane crashes, mistakes in surgery, etc.). His findings can be applied to mistakes we make whenever we do something challenging. Luckily, the mistakes you make don't have any serious consequences – at least not compared to an air crash.

If you want to accelerate the speed at which you get good at something, it helps if you do the following:

1 Make mistakes. This may sound obvious but some students feel frightened or depressed when they make mistakes, so they avoid making them. If a piece of work is difficult and they are likely to make lots of mistakes, they copy someone else's or 'forget' to hand it in. You must make mistakes so you can learn from them.

2 Once the error is made, grab it. Mistakes are information. Don't ignore them, hide them or quickly correct them. Study them.

3 Categorise your mistake and work out why it happened. Professor Reason argues that there are three broad reasons for error:

Type of mistake	Possible response
1. Active mistake The wrong process is carried out (e.g. the calculation goes wrong because an incorrect approach is used, the mark scheme isn't present, the student doesn't know what to do to get a high mark).	Examine processes. Categorise them. Attach processes to problems – are you using the right one?
2. Slip-up The correct process is chosen but errors in the execution of that process lead to a lower mark (e.g. a paragraph lacks detail or is missing a key component, a science or maths solution works up to a point and then breaks down).	Practise the process. Collect examples of the process being done well.

Type of mistake	Possible response
3. Blackout The information needed to complete the challenge is either missing or forgotten.	Review notes and knowledge. Check another student's notes. Use course textbooks to strengthen learning. Strengthen recall through revision techniques.

Try categorising your errors, then draw up a list of actions you could take to reduce the chances of that error occurring again.

32. Practice Activity: Mechanical vs. Flexible

A recent experiment undertaken with students at the Blue Coat School has a lot to tell us about practice.

All the students were set the same task – they had to throw a rolled-up ball of paper into a bin from three yards. They all knew they had to practise and that they would be tested on the number of successful throws they achieved at the end of the practice period. Here's the interesting bit: group 1 were told to repeat three yard throws over and over again, and group 2 were made to alternate between two yard and four yard throws over and over again.

When the two groups were brought back together to do a three yard bin throw, it's worth pointing out that group 1 had done hundreds of three yard bin throws. Group 2 hadn't practised any three yard bin throws at all.

Which was more successful? Group 2. Why? There is a difference between mechanical practice and flexible practice. Mechanical practice doesn't change – it repeats the same thing over and over. Flexible practice builds in different levels of challenge; the two yard throw is easier and the four yard throw is significantly harder.

What Does This Mean for A Level Study?

Those students who practise mechanically (group 1 students) can have nightmare exam experiences. They will often say, 'The question was slightly different! It totally messed with my concentration! I didn't know what to do!'

Students who practise flexibly (group 2 students) start to think flexibly. They will say, 'The questions were a bit weird. Eventually I worked out what I needed to do though.'

Make sure you mix it up in practice. Challenge yourself to:

» Seek out the weirdest questions that have ever come up and try them.

» Create strange questions.

» Visit the website of a different exam board and try their questions instead.

Do it this week. Stay flexible!

There is a difference between mechanical practice and flexible practice.

5. Attitude

> **Most people know that they really want to change, yet they just can't get themselves to do it.** Robbins (1992), p. 124

What Is Attitude?

Simply put, attitude is a settled way of thinking. The key adjective here is settled – that is, established over a period of time and sufficiently embedded to colour a person's perception of anything that might happen to them. We think of attitude as an umbrella term which includes a number of sub-factors, so when we talk about a student's attitude we generally mean:

» Their process of learning (i.e. the presence or absence of a growth mindset).

» Their buoyancy and positivity.

» Their response to challenge or difficulty.

» Their resilience and, of course, their grit.

Measuring and Changing

A fundamental challenge with attitude is how you measure it. There are now a number of questionnaires available that have been used to measure aspects of attitude. The problems associated with the use of self-report questionnaires have been well documented and these issues might be more significant where young people are concerned (see Fan et al., 2006). Notwithstanding these considerations, we've found questionnaires to be a useful tool when attempting to identify students who might need support.

Four questionnaires that we would recommend are Duckworth's 12-Item Grit Scale, Dweck's mindset questionnaire, the MTQ48 psychometric measure and, of course, the A Level Mindset questionnaire. The Grit Scale questionnaire, developed by Duckworth et al. (2007), is a paper-based test that is quick to administer and interpret. It can be a useful tool to use when working with students on vision – for example, we've used tutorial time to administer the questionnaire and informally discuss the results. The same applies to Dweck's mindset questionnaire, although this is considerably simpler.*

The MTQ48, developed by Clough et al. (2002), is a forty-eight item test that identifies levels of commitment, control, challenge and confidence. We've found this test very useful when designing targeted interventions as it provides a whole cohort overview of students' characteristics.

Finally, we have developed an A Level Mindset questionnaire. This identifies which aspects of the VESPA model where a student is strong and, more importantly, which areas might need to be developed. Details of the online test can be found at www.alevelmindset.com.

Once you've had a go at quantifying or measuring attitude, your next challenge lies in trying to change it. Shifting a student from a fixed to a growth mindset might sound straightforward in principle, but it will often involve a number of repeated interventions over a period of time. In the same way that changing an organisation's culture needs a cycle of repeated messages and corrections to behaviour, so any attitude change will require repeated inputs and corrections.

The research around changing student attitude is still in its infancy. Many of the strategies and tools available are experimental in nature and lack any real evidence, but it's likely that we will see much more development and research within this field over the next few years.

Many of the tools we've tried appear to elicit some change, but they don't work for everyone. In this chapter, more than any other, your understanding of your students is crucial. Look through the activities carefully and tailor them to specific cases. We rarely deliver these activities to large groups of students. Attitude emerges from a complex network of personal idiosyncrasies, and a coaching model is, we believe, the best way to surface and explore them.

---

* Duckworth's Grit Scale questionnaire can be found online at: https://sites.sas.upenn.edu/duckworth/pages/research and Dweck's mindset questionnaire at: http://mindsetonline.com/testyourmindset/step1.php.

> **Given the increasing research showing that mental toughness is a crucial factor in achieving academic outcomes and enhanced wellbeing [Clough and Strycharczyk, 2012], it is important that schools and educational institutions more broadly identify evidence-based approaches to support the development of mental toughness in young people.**
> Clough and Strycharczyk (2014), p. 96

Growth Mindset

Having a growth mindset (Dweck, 1999) has been a constant theme throughout this book. We believe it's crucial to student success. The attitudes of fixed mindset students mean they are unable to thrive under challenging conditions. They will use stories to explain why they can't do something. These narratives 'explain' success or failure in terms of genetic predisposition; gifts or talents that have been magically bestowed, or withheld, and focus on the endless abilities of a lucky few versus the finite resources left for the rest of us. These narratives are powerful and make a withdrawal of effort seem an entirely logical and pragmatic response to difficult work.

We've found that an effective way to deliver the growth mindset message is to get students to teach it. We start by delivering a lecture on the theory of growth mindset and sharing some real life stories to help them contextualise the concept. We then ask A level students to deliver a mindset lesson to Key Stage 3 learners. In this way, the message gets reinforced and deepened in our A level students, plus younger pupils get some exposure to mindset early in their academic career.

But mindset change takes more than a single session. Often the same message, dressed up in different ways and illustrated with different examples or attached to different stories, needs repeating over and again. Through assemblies, we will find ways of debunking myths about, for example, overnight success (every apparent 'overnight' success is grounded in years of preparatory work), effortless mastery (actually the result of very focused and deliberate practice) or right-place-right-time luck (a version of events which breezily disregards the countless right-place-wrong-time stories that have preceded success).

Once you begin thinking in these terms, examples will offer themselves up. Share them!

Buoyancy

Martin and Marsh (2009) have developed the concept of buoyancy to describe how students deal with everyday academic setbacks in the course of ordinary school life. We've all seen students who have received a bad grade and suddenly believe they can't do the subject. On the other hand, we know students who get a disappointing grade and are waiting outside your office door to get more feedback and then rush off to complete the work again.

The media abounds with uplifting stories of individuals who have shown exceptional levels of buoyancy. Every person who has ever been successful will have failed at some point in their life, and usually on an epic scale.

A good place to start here might be the list now commonly referred to as the 'Lincoln failures', which is a very clear and visual way to illustrate determined and repeated effort in the face of setbacks. It's a list of the personal and professional setbacks experienced by Abraham Lincoln on his journey to the position of president of the United States. Its accuracy is much discussed and debated by political historians, but it nevertheless offers a compelling example of persistence in the face of challenge.

Resilience

In simple terms, resilience is the ability to deal effectively with stress. This can be particularly relevant to A level students who are going through periods of high stress, especially during the exam season. There is some evidence to suggest that resilience has a positive correlation with academic success (Putwain et al., 2013). This is about helping

students with emotional control, particularly around anxiety and exams.

We know, as teachers, that worrying a little can often have a positive effect, as long as you don't pass a certain point. Worry can be a call to action – a nagging sense that something needs to be done. We've found that anxiety tends to reduce once action begins and that students are happier once they've crossed the threshold between contemplating and doing. After that point, however, worrying usually makes things worse. In order to counter excessive worrying, we introduce students to ideas about circles of influence and control, we share with them Dr Steve Peters' (2012) work on managing the inner chimp and we explore mindfulness. Like mindset, resilience develops through repeated ideas and messages. Once is not enough.

Teacher Guidance for Attitude Activities

33. Force Field Analysis

Big challenges can leave some students feeling overwhelmed. Revision, for example: they kind of want to do it but they don't. This is a coaching activity in which students assess their attitude towards a particular challenge (e.g. starting revision) and record their thought patterns and motivations in two columns: positive forces that justify the importance of the challenge, and negative forces that discourage them from engaging with it or giving it their full attention. They will need time to consider what obstacles they're coming up against and why they're finding this or that particular challenge hard to face or complete, and the space and time to honestly record their thinking.

The Force Field Analysis works a treat for procrastinators. It's one of those rare attitude activities that works well with a group, particularly with small groups of students who have been finding starting revision a challenge.

Some guidance here: your job is to coach students through the activity and change their attitude towards it. If you leave very negative students to do this piece of work alone, they will find enough reasons to reinforce that negative thinking. So be there when they do it and coach them into positivity. Your job is to generate, alongside them, a list of positive forces that are going to get them forging forward. You will need to be unflappable and creative. If you need help, choose positive students to deliver the session with you.

34. Stopping Negative Thoughts

A session where students have the opportunity to look at an important piece of research on negative thinking. There is some information to read through, introducing Albert Ellis' categories of crooked ('negative') thinking, and giving examples of these

thoughts expressed. Students will recognise themselves in these examples and are shown ways of reframing these thoughts. They then get a chance to coach an imaginary student with very negative thoughts, helping them to reframe their thinking.

A few names are probably already jumping into your mind of students who you would like to do this activity with – there is typically at least one in every class. We all know that it's usually a confidence issue, but it's worth making an effort to try to stop students using this type of language as it can lead to a self-fulfilling prophecy if left unchecked. It can also influence other students – something you must avoid at all costs!

This activity has transformed some of our discussions. When you're working with negative students, you can often begin to think that it's solely your responsibility to build some positivity for them. They might say, 'I'm terrible at this. I can't do it.' We used to respond with, 'No, you're not. You're great! You can do it!' But it doesn't work. All you've done is set yourself up in opposition to the student. Their feelings of failure are real and tangible. A chest thumping team-talk from you won't lift their mood. Instead, you need to draw their attention to the type of thinking on show.

We try to make this a light-hearted activity by showing the student a list of 'crooked thinking' and asking them if they recognise any patterns in their own language. Usually students are quickly able to identify their patterns. We know when we've done this activity well because we end up with previously negative students commenting, as they begin an account of a fresh crisis, 'I know, I'm catastrophising, but …' And that's a step forward.

If you want to go deeper with this activity, try getting students to complete the second part of the task and then get them to reframe their own thoughts. But begin by asking them to commit their negative thoughts to paper first. The act of writing down their negative comments can sometimes be enough to make them realise how illogical they sound.

35. Kill Your Critic

This is a simple list of suggestions for tackling a particularly strident inner voice whose message is undermining and negative. You will need a week to complete it, and the students will need to record the voice of their inner critic and practise challenging it.

Some interesting discussions have emerged from this activity. Sometimes this critical voice can give some sound advice. But when we continually doubt ourselves, the negative voice can be continuously spinning around in our head. In cognitive behavioural therapy they call this 'stinky thinking'.

This is one that's useful to give to students to read and then allow them some time for self-reflection. Send them home with it and meet them later once they've had time to digest and reflect.

36. There and Back

This is a homework activity which requires students to spend a portion of their independent time recording some thoughts and observations. They should take a forty minute walk and complete the activity during that period, so you will need to help them choose a route to a point twenty minutes away (there and back). When it works well, they will return to you with two lists: a positive list created during the first half of their walk and a negative list written during the second half.

Your coaching conversation will begin with something to celebrate and then move on to the challenges for which they will need to find solutions. The aim, as we're sure you can see, is perspective. Challenges and worries are offset against positives, so students feel a lot more balanced.

There is a health warning with this one, though. It's the Marmite of VESPA tools. Some students have been genuinely grateful and positive for the experience. But it's best to use this one only with students you know well; we've had some great results, sure, but we've also had the odd student who's just never come back!

37. Failing Forwards

In this activity we explore John Maxwell's assertion in *Failing Forward* (2012) that students respond to failure in two very distinct and different ways. For some, failure decelerates progress because it reinforces negative beliefs. For others, failure accelerates progress. Students have the opportunity to look through Maxwell's research, then consider their own response to failure in light of it. They will need the chance to reflect on recent failures and record how those experiences have changed their attitude.

This is a great activity to do with a student who is experiencing failure for the first time and is struggling to come to terms with the fact that they've got their first ever D grade in maths, for example. It's a great tool for getting students to think differently about how they approach the fact that they are not quite there yet.

When done well, you're establishing a framework that they can return to the next time they get a knock-back. Like many of these attitude activities, it works well if you accompany them with stories of famous failure. We begin one assembly with each member of the team admitting to their worst ever mistake, then telling students what they learned from it. Like so much of character education, we teach attitude by modelling it.

38. The Change Curve

This hand-out takes students through Elisabeth Kübler-Ross' Change Curve – a visual representation of people's emotional response to grief – and then asks students to consider their own emotional responses to the trauma of A level study. There are a number of examples that might stimulate discussion and a chance for them to discuss what they've found hard about A level study.

We share the Change Curve with all students at the very start of the academic year. The reason for this is we feel that it explains the journey of a student as they travel through the sixth form. Sharing this with students shows them that the path won't necessarily be straightforward, although we hope it will be. For most, there will be times when they are feeling low, anxious or just lost in what Kübler-Ross calls the 'emotional fog'. The good news is that they can return again and again to the curve, and remind themselves that they will come through it!

39. The Vampire Test

This activity encourages students to think about the influence of their peers, based on the interesting assertion that as you grow, you become the person who is the average of the five people you spend most time with. We like this as a way of approaching the idea of peer group influence.

Our research found that students often normalise their behaviour by surrounding themselves with individuals who are performing at a similar level to them. When we did the initial research for the A Level Mindset project we were particularly struck by the case of the two students with the lowest attendance in the sixth form. They had come from two different schools on the opposite sides of Manchester. They didn't know each other when they arrived, but after three weeks they had managed to find each other and were skipping lessons together, normalising and justifying their new patterns of behaviour. But there is the flipside too: those hugely successful students who buddy up with those who are just ahead of them, hitching a ride on their coat-tails and stretching themselves every day.

The Vampire Test takes a sideways look at the influence of peers, and encourages students to at least consider and acknowledge the effect of their friendship choices. Needless to say, this is a coaching activity to be completed with a single student only; other students shouldn't be named.

One way in to this activity that we've found useful is to first discuss friendship groups at an earlier stage of their educational career. The discussion can start like this:

» 'Can you tell me about a time when you had a friend who used to get you into trouble?' or

» 'Have you ever had a friend who made you a better person? Why? How?'

» Then move on to: 'Tell me about your current friends …' You can perhaps make comparisons from this point.

40. Stand Tall

The work of Amy Cuddy on power posing has become popular since her 2012 presentation, and is now among the most viewed TED talks. Cuddy's research focuses on how a change in posture can increase feelings of confidence and self-esteem and reduce feelings of fear. We've used this technique a number of times with students suffering from anxiety just before examinations.

This activity works particularly well as an assembly. We've shown sections of Cuddy's TED talk and then had the whole sixth form adopt power poses!

33. Attitude Activity: Force Field Analysis

Force Field Analysis is a method for listing, discussing and assessing the various forces for and against a proposed challenge you are facing. It helps you look at the big picture by analysing all of the forces impacting on you and weighing up the pros and cons. Having identified these, you can then develop strategies to reduce the impact of the opposing forces and strengthen the supporting forces. So, if you are finding it difficult to motivate yourself towards a certain aspect of your studies, this might be one for you.

Forces that help you achieve the challenge are called 'driving forces'. Forces that work against the challenge are called 'restraining forces'. Chart the forces by listing, in strength scale, the driving forces on the left and the restraining forces on the right. The important thing to do is to make sure the driving forces are more compelling than the restraining forces.

Have a go with a challenge you're facing.

The Challenge

Driving forces ➡	Current state	⬅ Restraining forces

34. Attitude Activity: Stopping Negative Thoughts

In his 1998 book, *How to Stubbornly Refuse to Make Yourself Miserable About Anything*, American psychologist Albert Ellis looked at irrational and negative thinking experienced by people in times of stress. He particularly looked at types of thoughts that people experience when things go badly. He called this 'crooked thinking'.

His work can be directly applied to students in stressful situations – see if you've experienced these kinds of thoughts when things go wrong:

» Not fair thinking: 'I don't deserve this treatment. Things shouldn't be like this.'

» Catastrophe thinking: 'If this goes wrong, it'll be a total nightmare.'

» Stopper thinking: 'I'm useless. I can't do this. I'm bound to screw up.'

» Illogical thinking: 'If this bad thing happens, this one will surely follow.'

» Blaming thinking: 'It's his fault. It's everyone's fault except me.'

» Overgeneralising: 'I never get the breaks. This always happens to me. Everything is going wrong in my life.'

Ellis argued that the first step was for the individual to recognise when they were slipping into negative thinking. Once they could do that, his suggestion was 'reframing the thought positively'. He said this meant being hard on yourself. Only one person could be in charge of your thoughts – you. So you have to be firm, strong and not take any nonsense.

» Not fair thinking becomes: 'I did what I could. It's a setback but I can handle it.'

» Catastrophe thinking becomes: 'I'm going to perform well. I'm well prepared.'

» Stopper thinking becomes: 'I'm learning. I'm getting better each time I hit a challenge like this.'

» Illogical thinking becomes: 'There's no direct connection between this and that. The past does not equal the future. Tomorrow's another day.'

» Blaming thinking becomes: 'It's happened now. It doesn't matter whose fault it was. The important thing is to move on and learn from it.'

» Overgeneralising becomes: 'There are a few problems I'm dealing with at the moment. Everyone has tough times and I'm no exception. But I know I'm strong enough to cope.'

Coaching Exercise

These are the kinds of thoughts you might find yourself, or hear others, expressing in difficult times. Take the statements below and see how you might reframe them into something more positive:

» I've never been good at exams.

» Stuff like this always happens to me.

» If my report is bad, my mum and dad are going to hate me.

» I'm only going to fail, so what's the point in trying?

» The teacher doesn't like me.

» Nothing goes right for me. Why should geography be any different?

» I've been rubbish at science since primary school. I should have never picked it for an A level.

» I'm not going to get the grades to get into university, so I'll end up without a job and have a miserable life.

» If I fail this mock, it will mean the whole term has been a disaster.

» This is typical of my life. Nothing is easy or straightforward. I'm sick of it.

35. Attitude Activity: Kill Your Critic

Popular psychology regularly refers to the 'inner critic' – the voice we all have inside our heads that pokes fun at our achievements, hopes and dreams. Some people have inner critics with such strong voices that they are too scared to commit to anything – we've worked with students who couldn't bring themselves to admit (even to a teacher or parent) what their dream or goal was.

If this is you, try the following activities to improve your confidence in yourself. Killing your critic isn't easy, but there are some ways forward.

» Name your critic. Seriously. Some students find it easier to dismiss the voice if they've given it a silly name.

» Listen to it – recognise its voice. Next time you hear it, label it: 'That's my inner critic.' At least you will start recognising it.

» Kill all comparisons. Let the inner critic say what it wants for ten minutes but all comparisons are banned. If it tries telling you, 'You're not as good as …' shut it down. It's called 'impostor syndrome' when you feel you are a fraud. 'I don't deserve to be here' or 'Others are cleverer than me' are common feelings and messages. Refuse to accept the voice if it tries any comparisons like these.

» Challenge your inner critic with data, such as your GCSEs or the last grade you got on a piece of work. Or challenge your inner critic with a demand: 'Well, if you think that, what should I do about it? Got any ideas?'

» Start working on something new but tell your inner critic you're just messing about. This is apparently a tactic used regularly in advertising and movie writing. You say to yourself, 'I'm just messing around here, making a few sketches or writing a few words. It's just a bit of fun …'

» Invite it to come back at another time. This is a good one. You say, 'I'd appreciate your constructive criticism when this is finished.' Set a date and write it down. Say to yourself, 'I'll listen to my critic – in a week's time for fifteen minutes.'

36. Attitude Activity: There and Back

This activity has been used successfully with adults experiencing difficulties in their work or personal life. It's a balancing exercise that frees up the mind and lets you make sense of hundreds of competing thoughts, ideas, worries and fears. So, if you're in a muddle, if you're struggling to feel positive or if you're feeling gloomy, this one might work for you.

The human brain works more effectively with good blood flow, so walking is essential to this activity. After your walk, you will need half an hour to collect your thoughts, jotting things down and making notes. Alternatively, you can use the voice recorder on a mobile phone to record your thoughts and ideas as you go. For this activity to work, you need to be disciplined and follow these rules to the letter!

Block out an hour of your time. You must be alone and undisturbed for this hour. Choose a destination that is about twenty minutes' walk away. While you walk there, you can only think positive thoughts. Your topic is: things I am good at and things I am thankful for. Nothing else can enter your mind. Bully yourself into staying on these two topics. Record your thoughts or list them quickly on a notepad.

Then turn around and return to your start point. While you walk back, you can address the problems you think you have, but here is the rule – your topic is: things I can do to solve my problems. Be strong with yourself. This is the only thing you can think about. When you arrive back, take a few minutes alone and make a note of your thoughts and ideas.

A final thought: worry is a call to action. If you're worrying, make a list of actions and then act on what you have listed. If you don't change things, things don't change.

Some people repeat this activity a couple of times a month to help them refocus. One person we know has the top of a hill as their destination – they say that walking down it helps them to relax after the hard slog of getting to the top, and they always come up with actions they can take to solve problems on the way down.

37. Attitude Activity: Failing Forwards

American journalist Dan Coyle (author of *The Talent Code* and *The Little Book of Talent*) argues that mistakes are information. He says that those who have become brilliant at something have got better at it quickly because they have made a lot of mistakes and they have paid attention to their mistakes and drawn the learning out from them.

So, failure is important if we are ultimately going to succeed. There are, however, different attitudes to failure. Some students hate it and avoid it at all costs. It makes them feel embarrassed, humiliated, worthless. They hide mistakes, don't complete tests or skip hard homework so they can avoid failing. As a result they make slower progress.

Other students recognise the importance of failure. Your job is to try to become one of these people. John Maxwell puts it this way in his book *Failing Forward* (2012): some people fail backwards (the failure takes them in a backwards direction), whereas some people fail forwards (the failure accelerates their progress).

Have a look at the characteristics Maxwell associates with these different types of failing in the table below.

Failing backwards	Failing forwards
Blaming others.	Taking responsibility.
Repeating the same mistake.	Learning from each mistake.
Expecting never to fail.	Knowing failure is part of the process.
Expecting to fail continually.	Maintaining a positive attitude.
Accepting tradition blindly.	Challenging outdated assumptions.
Being limited by past mistakes.	Taking new risks.
Thinking 'I am a failure'.	Believing something didn't work.
Withdrawing effort.	Persevering.

Now try to adapt your thinking so that it takes in the statements from the right-hand column.

» Take a recent failure and describe it in a paragraph. It might be a test, essay or homework that went badly.

» Now look at your teacher's feedback. What are they picking out as areas of weakness? Make some notes about this, rephrasing their feedback in your own words.

» Finish by making a simple list: what are you going to do differently next time?

38. Attitude Activity: The Change Curve

The Change Curve is based on a model originally developed in the 1960s by psychologist Elisabeth Kübler-Ross to explain the phases people go through during the grieving process. Kübler-Ross proposed that a terminally ill patient would progress through certain stages of grief when informed of their illness. Nowadays, the curve is used to help people understand their reactions to significant change in their lives.

Starting A level study is a significant change in any student's life and, like any change, it's likely that you will experience some of the following feelings.

The Change Curve

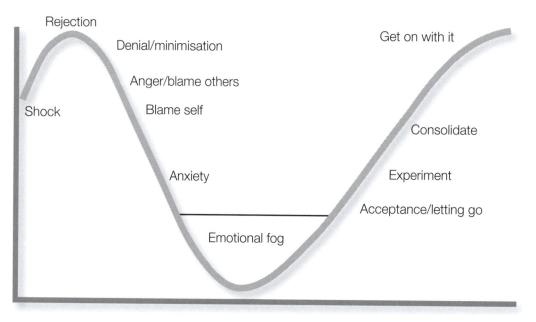

Think about your responses to A level. We've heard things like this:

» **Rejection:** 'I don't believe what you're telling me about A level study. It doesn't seem any different. I'll carry on as normal.'

» **Denial/minimisation:** 'I'm fine. It'll be alright. Stop hassling me about how different it is.'

» **Anger:** 'I actually hate this. The teachers are rubbish. The subjects are nothing like they said they would be. I wish I'd never started or gone to that other college.'

» **Blame self:** 'It turns out I'm just not clever enough to do this.'

» **Anxiety:** 'Everyone else is better than me. I'm missing deadlines. I'm not sleeping well. I don't understand the work. I'm not enjoying this challenge at all. I'm scared I'll fail.'

» **Emotional fog:** Withdrawing effort. Giving up.

» **Acceptance/letting go:** 'Things are different now. It's hard, but I'm getting to grips with it.'

» **Experiment/consolidate/get on with it:** 'I'm getting better at this. My grades aren't great but they're improving. There are some parts of these courses I like.'

How does this help? First, you're not alone. Everyone goes through these feelings. Acknowledge and accept them. Second, some students go faster than others, but for most people it takes until the spring to get through the fog. Third, wherever you are on the curve, keep your eyes on the next stage. You *will* get there!

You are the average of the five people you spend the most time with.

Jim Rohn

39. Attitude Activity: The Vampire Test

Jim Rohn is an entrepreneur and writer who studies success. In essence, he argues that those who surround themselves with good people become good – those who surround themselves with hard working people become hard working. Equally, those who surround themselves with lazy people become lazy.

This is something we see every year: promising students who have a friendship group which almost enforces disengagement. The group will effectively mock or punish any group member who is enjoying study, succeeding or working hard. It's sometimes difficult to tell if it's happening to you, and by the time you've figured it out it can be too late.

Taking the Test

Writer and artist Austin Kleon has a solution. He calls it the Vampire Test, and he explains it in his book, *Show Your Work!* Kleon advises that 'if, after hanging out with someone you feel worn out and depleted, that person is a vampire. If, after hanging out with someone you still feel full of energy, that person is not a vampire' (2014, p. 129).

Think about the five people you spend most time with and ask yourself five questions about them:

» Are they positive people?

» Do they enjoy their lives?

» Are they a good influence?

» Have they helped you through problems?

» Do they make you feel good about yourself and about life?

If you answer 'no' to these questions, can you list the names of people who might be better students to spend time with?

40. Attitude Activity: Stand Tall

If you're a football fan, what do you do when your team scores a goal? What do you do if you win when playing a game or listening to your favourite band? For most people the answer is to stand up tall with their arms outstretched – something similar to the pose you often see Usain Bolt adopt as he crosses the 100 metre finish line.

Amy Cuddy, a social psychologist at Harvard University, has looked at why people adopt this pose and the effects it can have on your physiology. She has found that by changing your physiology (or your posture) you can have a profound effect on how you feel. In her 2012 TED talk, 'Your Body Language Shapes Who You Are', she argues that by standing in certain 'power poses' you can increase your confidence and self-esteem, enhance your memory and reduce feelings of fear.

Cuddy goes on to argue that weaker postures (such as curling up, making yourself small or moving into defensive positions) trigger other psychological responses – feelings of imminent danger, stress or threat. And yet we often see nervous students hunched over their notes or hiding in a corner in those last few moments before an exam!

Instead, we think it's worth trying more confident and powerful postures before taking your final exams or important assessments.

Here's how you do it ...

Power Pose 1

Stand tall with your hands on your hips and elbows pointing out. Your feet should be approximately one foot apart. Look straight ahead and think of a time you felt confident, strong and in control. Hold the pose for as long as you can. Aim for five minutes. You may need to begin with two or three minutes and build up.

Power Pose 2

You will need a little more space for this one. Stand as above, but this time put your arms above your head, stretched out like the arms of a clock at the 10 to 2 position. Again, hold your head high, stick your chest out and think about a time you felt really confident. And again, if you can, hold the pose for five minutes.

These poses are positive and confidence building – but not ones you might feel comfortable doing in public. Therefore, don't think of this as an activity you can only do outside an exam hall. We've found standing tall can also benefit students when they hit a block in their revision.

So, next time you're working away in your room and you hit a block, don't hunch yourself over your notes. Take a break and stand in the power pose!

Footnote: Our Delivery

What follows is a brief exposition of our current VESPA curriculum. It's far from perfect and it's developing all the time. There are elements we're starting to feel really pleased with and mistakes we're still making. But, for what it's worth, it looks like this:

» **The lecture programme.** Every two weeks we deliver a whole year group lecture for one hour. We gather 200-odd students together all at once, sitting in their forms, which allows us to communicate a consistent message. There will be an aspect of the A Level Mindset VESPA model within the lecture. We cover effort early in Year 12, exploring the differences between proactive and reactive independent study. We do a lecture on systems, demonstrating the key principles and using videos of students talking about the challenges of organising their resources and time. Another Year 12 autumn term staple is a lecture on different types of universities, encouraging students to develop vision early in the year. There will be activities that the students do en masse – including some of the resources in this book.

» **Assemblies.** We run a weekly assembly with each year group which lasts for fifteen minutes. It usually has an implicit rather than overt VESPA message and is delivered, like most assemblies, through storytelling.

It is useful to bring the five elements of the model to life by focusing on real life stories of success and failure.

» **Tutorials.** Our tutors effectively design their own A Level Mindset curriculum – they specify an element of the model for a particular week and then choose an activity from those available. If week 3 is vision, for example, some might go for Your 21st Birthday while others might choose Twenty Questions. We watch these sessions being delivered – and it's regularly one of the highlights of the week.

A year might look something like the curriculum opposite. There are some anomalies specific to our context – mysterious gaps in December and March which are explained by whole school events and activities that our students might be taking part in or playing a role in leading. Though there are only ten activities in this scheme, we are just as likely to cover twelve or more per year. The remainder are used for cohort-specific interventions.

The A Level Mindset Curriculum

Week	VESPA component	Activity
Week 2 – September	Vision	Your 21st Birthday
Week 4 – September	Effort	Working Weeks
Week 2 – October	Systems	Snack, Don't Binge (or the Weekly Review)
	Half-term	
Week 1 – November	Attitude	Failing Forwards
Week 3 – November	Attitude	Stopping Negative Thoughts
	Christmas	
Week 1 – January	Vision	Fix Your Dashboard
Week 3 – January	Effort	The 1–10 Scale
Week 2 – February	Practice	The Revision Questionnaire
	Half-term	
Week 2 – March	Systems	STQR/The Energy Line
Week 4 – March	Practice	Know the Skills
	Easter	

6. Coaching

'Having a Word'

'Don't worry, we'll have a word with them.' We are slightly embarrassed to admit that this is something we've said many times to tutors who have requested support with underperforming students. Here's the bad news: in our experience, 'having a word' with a student does not lead to an improvement in academic performance. Yes, you might see a brief change in behaviour, but does a chat really impact on performance?

So what might you do when faced with the problem of a student who, for whatever reason, isn't engaging with study or succeeding? If having a word isn't the answer, what is? We've found that adopting the principles of coaching can be incredibly powerful.

The key principle of coaching is to unlock the coachee's potential and to help them to maximise their own performance – that is, guide them to a series of actions that will help them achieve their goal. The concept is not a new one – it has been used in sport and business for many years. It has not been easy to demonstrate the effectiveness of coaching within education through empirical research, although there is some evidence that has shown the impact of coaching on Year 12 students (Campbell and Gardner, 2005). We are cautious when it comes to ascribing student success to the coaching conversations that support them; there are so many variables impacting on a student's life that it is hard to be certain. But without doubt we've seen a greater capacity for self-reflection and regulation in our coachees.

Excellent coaching doesn't just happen. It's a skill that takes training and practice to develop. Research we have conducted shows that often teachers don't feel confident about coaching in one-to-one situations, so it might be worth doing a temperature check in your organisation to evaluate your starting point. We believe that proper training is crucial if you are going to embed a coaching culture. Like all good teaching and learning, the process is ongoing and needs a long-term strategy for it to be implemented successfully. We have invested a significant amount of time and resources to the coaching process, and we are confident that the return of investment far outweighs these considerations.

We started our coaching journey by using the GROW model (Whitmore, 2009). This model is used extensively in business and life coaching fields and can be very effective. The conversation opens with a student outlining their goal (G). Next comes a discussion of the current reality (R) – where the student is in relation to the goal right now. Following that, the conversation covers obstacles (O) that are currently impeding progress and generates solutions for avoiding these. Finally, the conversation agrees some ways forward (or will to succeed) (W).

We've had some real successes with the model. It has had a particular impact in developing cycles of discussion and reflection, which strengthens students' capacity to explore their own habits and behaviours and assess their impact on progress. But good coaching relies on the coachee being able to generate solutions to their own problems with only limited guidance. We found the GROW model didn't provide us with enough tools to help with behaviour change.

We have made much more significant gains through coaching students using the A Level Mindset approach to coaching – assessing and exploring student performance under the five VESPA headings – rather than using other coaching frameworks. Over a period of time and practice, we have become extremely effective at the diagnosis of student underperformance by identifying the root causes as resulting from one of the following causes:

» A lack of vision.

» Low levels of effort.

» Poor systems.

» Inadequate practice.

» A negative attitude.

Once that diagnosis has been made, we found we could use one of the forty VESPA activities described in the book. We weren't 'having a word' any more; we were getting students to do something tangible and return to us to discuss the results. For example, a student with low levels of effort might complete the Power of If … Then Thinking or one with malfunctioning systems might sit with us and complete the Energy Line. Used in this way, the VESPA tools have had huge impact on behaviour change.

Coaching Using the A Level Mindset VESPA Model

The diagram below represents a series of actions to take when you are faced with the challenge of turning around an underperforming student. There are a series of steps, each of which we will explain in further detail below. It's much more than having a word, and its impact is much greater too.

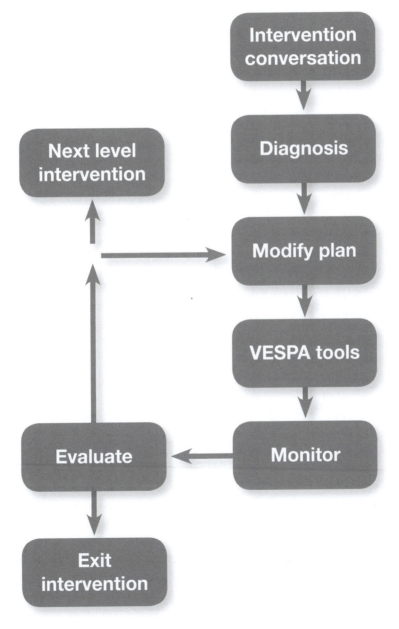

The Intervention Conversation: Asking Great Questions

We begin at the top of the flow chart with an 'intervention conversation'. These conversations with students are diagnostic – we are aiming to identify areas of the VESPA model where they are currently deficient. One way is to start by checking the students' vision and then working through each of the other elements in turn: effort, systems, practice and attitude. In this way you will begin to build up a picture of where the student's areas for development might be. This is where the real diagnosis takes place: where do you see the most significant problems?

A series of short and simple questions can take you to the heart of the difficulty. Asking great questions is key to unlocking self-awareness. By asking students questions that really make them think, the hope is that you will break down barriers and encourage them to take responsibility for their learning.

Below are some example VESPA questions that you could use during the intervention conversation:

» **Vision.** Where do you see yourself in two years' time, at the end of your sixth form studies? Do you have a clear idea about what career you want to pursue?

» **Effort.** How much time are you spending on studying? Are you performing to the best of your academic ability?

» **Systems.** Let's check your bag – are your files organised? When was the last time you missed a deadline? What was the reason? Can we look at how you're recording the tasks you need to do?

» **Practice.** How do you prepare for assessments? When was the last time you spent an hour or so completing a piece of work under exam conditions? Have you asked your teachers for feedback?

» **Attitude.** What motivates you to study? What are you enjoying about A level study? What are you finding uncomfortable?

Alternatively, for a more free-form approach, we've found that a single question can be an enlightening starting point: 'What aspects of A level study are you finding hard?' Try this with an underperforming student and listen carefully to their response. Students will regularly identify issues to do with vision, effort, systems, practice and attitude.

Whichever way you do it, make sure you keep a simple record of your conversation. This is important so that when you evaluate the student's progress, you have some notes and a record of the agreed action steps. Something as straightforward as a simple record sheet will help enormously.

Coach record sheet

	Notes	Action steps/tools	Priority
V			
E			
S			
P			
A			

Diagnosis and VESPA Activities

Our intervention conversation will flag up one (usually more, sometimes five!) areas for concern. Once we've identified the main obstacle, we have to decide where to begin. There are various approaches you can adopt. If a student is in crisis, we'll naturally need to start where the tension is – the root cause. Often this is vision. The process could be long but it will be worth it. Alternatively, if we're making smaller, incremental adjustments to performance, we might begin at the point where we can make either the quickest change or the highest impact change for the lowest cost.

We recommend that in your first session you only work on one or two areas. If you try to change too many behaviours at the same time, the student will likely fail. Behaviour change is often about altering habits and these are more likely to stick if undertaken in small steps.

The process from there is about selecting VESPA activities that can practically and measurably change student behaviour. Which tool you use will depend on your professional judgement about what you think might work best with the individual student. You can either work through the VESPA tools with the student or you might ask them to complete a task at home and bring it to the next session.

Monitoring, Evaluation and Modification

Like any good coaching conversation, you are aiming to end your first session with time-bound targets that can be discussed at your next meeting. Students need to leave the meeting with a clear, unequivocal record of their action steps. If they don't, all you've done is 'have a word'!

Make sure that the goals are SMART. By using a simple table, like the one below, the student knows what they have to do and when.

Student action steps

Action step	By when	Priority

Your subsequent aim is to catch students doing things right and begin celebrating those small steps forward. In order to do this effectively, it's important to give your students some time to change their behaviour. Through this period you simply monitor their performance, although you should have accurate and reliable tools for monitoring progress or it will be difficult to observe any changes. Use attendance, punctuality, behaviour logs, work submission and teacher feedback.

The time you leave between coaching sessions will depend on the student's issue(s). We recommend two weeks as a maximum. During the second conversation, you review how things have been going and modify the plan, if necessary. If things have gone well and you feel confident that the issue has been resolved, then the student might exit the intervention. If not, then you review the action steps and repeat the process using one of the VESPA tools. Depending on the student, this will usually determine the number of coaching sessions. We have had success with students after one session, whereas others have taken four or five.

Whatever the outcome, stick at it. There is always an inflection point – a moment where a student clicks, masters an element of their study or makes a significant step forward. Carol Dweck's persistent use of the word 'yet' is a reminder to us all that mastery takes time.

Don't label a young person by using language which doesn't allow for the possibility of change. Avoid, 'You're disorganised,' and instead go for, 'You haven't yet mastered some of the methods which will boost your levels of organisation.' 'Yet' offers up a world of possibilities. Your coaching conversations should do the same.

7. Making it Happen

This chapter is intended for readers who are interested in the process by which they might encourage and embed a large-scale application of the A Level Mindset VESPA model in their organisation – for example, you might be reading this as a middle manager or senior leader. If you are a coach or tutor who is happy to take specific elements of the model or activities to use in one-to-one conversations or to teach to a single group, you needn't read this chapter. The problems and possible solutions described here aren't things you need to worry about!

We explore the approaches you might make to sell the system to the school, overcome resistance from staff or students, influence a team of tutors, encourage teachers to get on-board or make a plan of action for implementing the entire system. We also describe how we have implemented the A Level Mindset in our own organisation and how we are continuing to try to embed it in our school. We have made our fair share of mistakes attempting to get it right, and it's not perfect yet. That said, if you are interested in our journey so far, read on. However, this section of the book comes with a health warning: it is not intended to be a guide to effective change management. There are plenty of far better qualified people to give you the lowdown on that!

Overcoming Resistance

If you are interested in embedding the A Level Mindset VESPA system in your organisation, you will probably encounter resistance to the idea. There will be staff who tell you it's unnecessary, unproven and unwieldy. Here, we offer a model for anticipating and planning for this kind of negative response. You might be familiar with Kathleen Dannemiller's formula for change (Dannemiller and Jacobs, 1992), adapted from earlier work by Richard Beckhard and Rubin Harris (1987). It's a neat way to think about large scale cultural and organisational change, and it's something we return to pretty regularly. It looks like this:

$$D \times V \times F > R$$

Dannemiller's argument is that successful change management understands the motivations beneath, and reasons for, organisational inertia and plans carefully to maximise the chances of overcoming that resistance.

Dissatisfaction (D) refers to people's awareness and understanding of the shortcomings of their current way of doing things. Part of successful change management is therefore about seeding and growing this sense of dissatisfaction. It may take some time and it will need data – concrete illustrations of weaknesses in current systems and structures.

Vision (V) is, of course, the compelling and clear new version of what might be. This needs to be both achievable and exciting, and it needs to pay homage to and incorporate the best elements of the previous system, not replace it wholesale.

First steps (F) refers to a series of executable actions which can be realistically taken to begin the journey towards the goal. Frameworked and exemplified first steps work best.

If each of these elements is strong, clear, memorable and compelling, together they will overcome whatever resistance (R) there is to change.

In this chapter, we will take you through each element of Dannemiller's formula and explore some possible actions you might want to consider if you're interested in embedding the system in your organisation. What follows is not in any way the correct way, the best way or the only way. It is simply a whole bunch of possibilities, some of which might work in your institution and context and some of which may not.

Surfacing Dissatisfaction – Three Places to Start

As Dannemiller's formula suggests, one of the ways you can encourage an awareness of the need for change is to seed dissatisfaction with the way things currently work. What follows are three activities you might want to consider, all of which are effective at exposing problems. They require you to gather staff together and elicit feedback about current systems of student support, monitoring, coaching and intervention. They worked for us because they gave us the data to demonstrate dissatisfaction with the existing system.

1. Glad, Sad, Mad

We found this activity incredibly useful when it was first introduced to us. It's so simple and straightforward to run but yields so much interesting stuff. Sit your teaching team down in groups. Make sure you get your groupings right so you've got a good balance of what we call 'problem spotters' and 'problem solvers'. (Lots of problem spotters together means you get too much bile and not enough brightness!)

Ask them to reflect on their work specifically as sixth form tutors (or teachers, progress champions, directors of learning – whatever your team might be), listing everything they can about their job that makes them feel either glad, sad or mad. This works well because of the different tone and feel provoked by the three adjectives.

The glad stuff captures some positivity which you can later share. It gives you the 'here are the things we're doing well and enjoying' list to celebrate. It is interesting to distinguish between the sad and the mad stuff. We've found that staff tend to be sad about immovable or irretrievable situations – the 'beyond our control' factors and issues. The mad category has, for us at least, borne the most fruit. Here, you will get observations about 'problems we could potentially fix but we haven't'. These observations are gold dust for seeding dissatisfaction. It will be tough to see a few of your own projects in there – systems, policies or procedures you might have been responsible for leading on. No matter. Set aside the ones that are non-negotiable and use the rest to begin to explore what it is that creates frustration. Feed it back.

Try this approach, for example: 'You've made it really clear that you're dissatisfied with the materials we're currently using in PSHCE. Can we explore that a bit further? What isn't working? What could be better? What would you like us to achieve in these sessions?' Once that dialogue is up and running you've got the start of a project. Put your best staff on it. Give them a steer towards the outcome you want. Check in regularly and contribute yourself. Shape it and nurture it.

2. Why Do Students Fail?

This remains a firm favourite with us because when we sat down together to create it, many of the issues that formed the A Level Mindset

VESPA model made themselves evident. We repeat this activity on training days – it's always an eye-opener.

Group your staff carefully, as before, then distribute a whole bunch of sticky notes and ask them to write down one reason why students fail their A level courses. Be clear on your definition of 'fail' – you might mean a grade U or you might mean 'fail to progress to Year 13' or 'significantly underperform'.

When your tables are festooned with sticky notes, ask staff to group them into the following categories:

» **Personal issues.** For the most part these are your intractables. Students might need, for example, involvement from specialists in other agencies or bespoke medical support. There will always be a proportion of these. Set them aside.

» **Cognitive judgement.** Separate out the ones where staff have expressed a personal opinion about students, such as 'They're not clever enough' or 'They're on the wrong course'. If there are a lot of these you've either got a mindset issue with staff or an enrolment issue. To check, use GCSE points scores as a rule of thumb. Look at other local providers to see what they require of students in order to enrol on courses and watch out for challenging combinations of what we call 'step based' courses – A levels that aren't just discrete topics but require mastery of one skill in order to access the next. (For us, these are maths and further maths, biology, chemistry, physics and languages.) If the issue is staff mindset, make a note of who you need to convert and start mindset training during team meetings.

» **What have you got left?** It will most likely be observations about student mindset: students not working hard enough, not being organised, not knowing why they're doing a course or what it's for, or students who don't revise properly.

Now you've got the information to get started. Try: 'We've got a list here of flaws and weaknesses in our learners that are preventing them from succeeding. What if we design a series of activities that help them to overcome these problems? Can we explore that a bit further? What would these tasks and activities look like? Who would like to help design some?'

If you get what our head teacher likes to call 'a coalition of the willing' together, you've got the start of a project.

3. The PSHCE Audit

Ask a small number of willing staff to interview students who have come to study with you from different schools in the area – get a range of previous providers if you can. If you're an 11–18 school, interview some of your own students and some who have joined you specifically for your Key Stage 5 provision. Your aim is to obtain a straightforward account of what this range of students have covered in PSHCE (or equivalent) during Key Stages 3 and 4. Then gather your team and together synthesise what you've got. For example, in Year 9 kids covered X and Y. In Year 10 they did Z. And so on. Some schools do PSHCE superbly well and it will be an interesting experience to see what students have covered, but, regrettably, schools like this tend to be in the minority.

More likely, if your experience is anything like ours, two points will emerge:

1 Some students will have done certain topics two or three times already because their previous schools might not have audited what they are covering year on year in PSHCE. So you will get lists that, understandably, include drugs, alcohol, STDs and cyber-bullying over and over again. Feed this back to your team; it frees you up to reconsider your provision. You don't need to cover this material in detail in the same way again. In an hour you can cover well-being and incorporate some or all of the above. Now you've got time to do other things – for example, developing vision, strengthening systems or some attitude work.

2 The PSHCE focus that students will have experienced thus far could well have been negative. Rather than a series of strategies for living well and being happy, students may well have sat through the delivery of a ton of information read from a list of evils to avoid: unhealthy eating, energy drinks, excessive screen-time, smoking. You've got a great opportunity here because your emphasis can be more positive. Your angle can be giving students strategies to make them less stressed and more productive, resilient, flexible, creative and happier.

Use your audit as the starting point for a discussion. Try: 'Students' experience of pastoral support has so far focused on sexual health and fitness. We don't need to cover these topics in detail again. What could we do with the time instead? Who would like to join a working party exploring what else we might offer?' In this way, as well as investigating the need for a new type of sixth form PSHCE experience, you are also giving staff the capacity (i.e. time) to deliver these activities *and* asking for their help in designing them.

Vision

The second element of Dannemiller's model is vision – ensuring you have a significant and compelling version of the future that staff can buy into. One way of approaching this is to engage staff in vision building.

Notice how our focus here is entirely on students.

Try giving your team the following sentence starter: 'We're going to improve students' ability to …' or 'We're going to develop students so they can …' Ask staff to complete the sentences. What you should get are verbs – actions, routines, habits and skills your staff want the students to be able to develop and successfully execute. You can keep a tally of the most popular habits and skills, crunch the data and then feed it back, thematically categorise it or choose a top ten – whatever you think will work best to focus your staff on developing students.

Notice how our focus here is entirely on students. In this case, it is worth making sure your vision is not prosaically performance based. Avoid, 'to achieve A level results that reflect …', 'to design a pastoral curriculum that …', 'to increase value-added in …' or, indeed, any of the other banal outcomes that might spring to mind. If your focus is on developing the students, then more positive outcomes will follow.

First Steps

Dannemiller points out that for a change management project to be successful, staff need more than just a sense of dissatisfaction and a vision for how they would like the future to be. They need a clear sense of where they are expected to start – what the first steps are.

Providing staff with the first steps to change means turning something that until now has been only abstract – a sense of dissatisfaction or a vision for a different future – into something much more concrete. You're going to need to give staff solid, practical and useful example resources and ideas. They are busy people, so if they are going to adjust the way they work, you need to make it easy for them.

There is one significant disadvantage to arriving with a fully formed, wholesale solution to a problem – it's got someone else's fingerprints all over it. So, your first steps offering should be a starting point: four or five great resources or activities with some observations and feedback on how they went, followed by an invitation to join a team tasked with designing some more. How do you get yourself into a position to do this? Try running a pilot study.

Pilots, Prototypes and Pioneers

A pilot study is a small scale test run of what you might want to do on a larger scale. Gather a group of willing volunteers to try out a small number of resources. They might be some of the A Level Mindset VESPA activities or they might be character development activities you've planned yourself. You might involve a small target group of underperforming students or a single tutor group. By running a small trial you can discover some of the challenges you might face, then rectify these before introducing the idea to a wider circle of staff.

A great strength of this approach is that it allows you to collect data using focus groups. As the teaching profession has become more research informed, teachers want evidence to support interventions before they begin delivery. Use a focus group to review and evaluate the potential strengths and weaknesses of the activities and sessions you've designed. Many of the activities we've included in the book have emerged from student focus groups and feedback sessions where a group of confident senior students have pulled apart their provision and suggested ways forward, or (in the case of, say, Twenty Questions) built activities alongside us by kicking out the content they don't like and keeping the stuff they do.

What your pilot study allows you to do is build a prototype. You're getting your innovation out there, watching it fail or succeed, and learning the lessons. Make adjustments if it all goes wrong, and do so cheerfully! If something isn't working and you're confident enough to point it out and remove or change it, your colleagues will see someone who is creative and flexible, someone who isn't pig-headed or precious about a particular idea or way of doing things. Prototyping has proved useful for us because there is a tendency in everyone – us included – to labour in secret, waiting until something is close to perfect

before letting anyone else see it. Weeks turn into months, months into years and 'that project' you've talked about is still in the third drawer down – the graveyard of a thousand good ideas.

The key to a good pilot study, and essential to building a robust and successful prototype, is involving the right people. Look for pioneers. Many schools already have a pioneer without realising it – they are sometimes called 'connectors' or 'influencers' in the business world. You simply find someone who is already doing the kind of work you want to see more widely and then champion them. Get them involved. It is sometimes more powerful for staff to hear success stories from colleagues rather than senior leaders.

Keeping It Simple

There is an internet adage we like: the solution must be simpler than the problem. The problem – the one you've been seeding dissatisfaction about – is a complex beast; your solution shouldn't be. So don't design a seventeen-step plan that will drive away all but the most committed. Start small and simple and your project will appear achievable. This doesn't mean you can't acknowledge the nuances and subtleties of what you are trying to do – of course you can. Don't let someone tell you that you haven't recognised the complexities of the issue. You have. It's just that in designing a solution, you have prioritised those issues which will give you high impact results.

If you're ever in doubt about where to start, try a simple prioritisation matrix like this one:

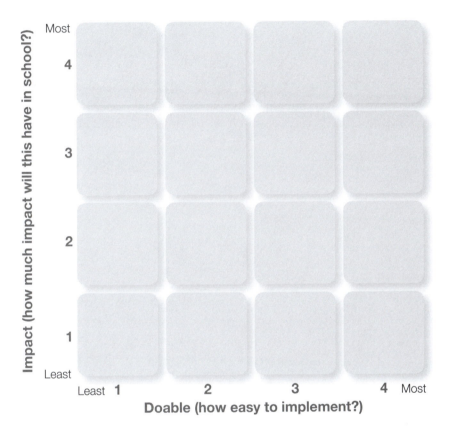

Some people refer to easy-to-do but low impact actions (bottom right of the grid) as 'low hanging fruit' and easy-to-do but high impact actions (top right of the grid) as 'quick wins'. Whatever you call them, get them done so you can move on to the actions that will begin to differentiate you from the organisations around you – those that are hard to achieve but reap rich rewards.

Conclusion

Ten Final Thoughts

There is far less of a significant link between exam results at 16 and success at A level than we might suppose. The past doesn't equal the future. That goes for the modest achiever who turns into a breakthrough learner at A level, and perhaps even more so for the high achiever who expects the same thing to happen again but hits the ceiling.

We believe there are five keys to success at A level and that these five elements – having a vision, making a habit of effort, building effective systems, engaging in high stakes practice and having the correct attitude – can be practised and learned.

Here's a useful metaphor to guide your thinking: we're used to the concept of avatars from computer gaming. Games ask us to assume the identity of another character, often one with certain strengths and weaknesses that need to be upgraded and developed if we are to be successful. When we have a psychological distance between gamer and avatar, we're happy to go about improving our character – getting more strength here, building intelligence there, developing skills and attributes as the game goes on. When it comes to self-improvement, however, we're much more reluctant and defensive. Learners find it hard to acknowledge and address their weaknesses.

Our job is to create a non-judgemental environment in which students can critically assess themselves and then support them in making improvements.

On Vision

1 Having a vision is central to success. It's the first element of the VESPA model because it's the most important. We're not here to judge a dream, just to encourage action towards it. Dreams become goals when you take action. You're not killing a dream by turning it into a goal, but some students may tell you otherwise. Turning a dream into a goal is a frightening prospect and some people prefer the safety of discussing dreams without ever doing anything about them.

2 Imagining your future self builds a sense of direction and having a positive visual dashboard maintains focus. This is particularly useful at key turning points in the academic calendar – for example, try encouraging the students to build a vision board in January.

On Effort

3 Effort is relative. Students who surround themselves with hard working people will get better grades. One way to crack this is to ensure that you raise the effort levels of the whole cohort. For this you need information about how hard working your highest achievers are. Once you have this information, share it. Normalise high levels of effort and build the habit. If students had a job they would be doing something like a thirty-eight hour working week. Most A level timetables at most institutions reach about twenty-two hours. Check what your students are doing on average and encourage them to top it up. There are those who might argue, 'These kids have got the rest of their lives for the drudgery of a 9 to 5. Why start them off on it now?' But work – *good* work – should be fascinating, engaging and positive, not drudgery. We are empowering students by giving them the freedom and confidence to choose their career path when they are older. Work can and should be a good thing.

4 We all have blockers. Those students who recognise their blockers – and acknowledge that these feelings of resistance and self-sabotage come from within – can unblock quicker. They work harder and get better grades. Study, like any challenge, is as much about mastering yourself as it is about mastering the subject.

On Systems

5 The phrase 'study skills' has proved pretty unhelpful for us. It's too nebulous and difficult to define. Instead, try this: A levels are projects and completing them

successfully needs project management skills. Anyone who has seen through the design and delivery of a big project will have, along the way, developed their own systems and processes for making sure that everything gets done by a deadline. But no one teaches us how to do this. Check out any bookshop and you will see shelves of self-help guides about productivity and organisation; even as professional adults we sometimes feel overwhelmed by everything we have to do. Now imagine you're 16! So a whole bunch of simple prioritisation tools can make a huge difference. Students will be calmer and happier. They will lead less cluttered lives.

6 If there is one quality that defines students with good systems, it's that they snack rather than binge. Little and often beats cramming hands down. That means subdividing tasks into component parts – in other words, chunking them. Chunking a task makes it far less scary and it makes self-assessment of progress easier. Regularly assessing the progress of individual projects allows students to adjust focus when necessary and it leads to better and more consistent results.

On Practice

7 Good exam preparation is a three step process: learning the content, developing skills and seeking feedback from experts. To be top performers in exams, students need to know the skills being tested. This will allow them to practise under a variety of conditions, building agility and flexibility. Practice can involve isolating the skill and strengthening it over and over again, without the high stakes associated with performing in exam conditions. A drill is a practice activity undertaken outside these conditions. Whatever skill you're focusing on, design drills that give students plenty of time, encouraging them to pay attention to each action they execute. Give them exemplars too and you will bring students on faster.

8 Successful students take action and practise hard. Hard practice is high stakes and it's uncomfortable. It's not something young learners are going to cleave to with a song in their hearts. You will need to pull them into that uncomfortable position to begin with and be patient while they get slightly more used to being there.

On Attitude

9 Successful students have to want to succeed more than they fear failure. Mistakes are crucial – failure is a necessary part of learning. Watch out for the perfectionist who has a narrative about themselves that goes, 'I never get less than an A. I never have to redo pieces. I never have to attend extra sessions.' As courses get tougher these students will hide their inability to live up to their story about themselves.

They will refuse help. Encourage students to fail and collect feedback – they will have so much useful information to work with.

10 By 16 or 17 students can start thinking about learning holistically and get used to using the meta-language of learning. They are ready to hear lively accounts, delivered by you or your team, about research into the importance of mindset, neuroplasticity, the power of practice, the psychology of positivity and resilience. Having a growth mindset – believing they can and will master their subjects – is the first step. Just telling your students about mindset will have an effect, but really engaging with and discussing the research will carry them further. Be unswerving and unconditional in your belief in them and in your commitment to help develop them.

They can't ask for more than that.

References

Ackerman, J. (2008). *Sex Sleep Eat Drink Dream: A Day in the Life of Your Body* (New York: Mariner Books).

Allen, D. (2002). *Getting Things Done: How to Achieve Stress-Free Productivity* (London: Piatkus).

Beckhard, R. and Harris, R. T. (1987). *Organizational Transitions: Managing Complex Change* (2nd edn) (Reading, MA: Addison-Wesley Publishing).

Belsky, S. (2011). *Making Ideas Happen: Overcoming the Obstacles Between Vision and Reality* (New York: Penguin).

Bloom, B. S. (ed.) (1985). *Developing Talent in Young People* (New York: Ballantine Books).

Campbell, M. A. and Gardner, S. (2005). A Pilot Study to Assess the Effects of Life Coaching with Y12 Students. In M. Cavanagh, A. M. Grant and T. Kemp (eds), *Evidence Based Coaching*, Vol. 1: *Theory, Research and Practice from the Behavioural Sciences* (Bowen Hills, QLD: Australian Academic Press), pp. 159–169.

Clough, P., Earle, K. and Sewell, D. (2002). Mental Toughness: The Concept and Its Measurement. In I. Cockerill (ed.), *Solutions in Sport Psychology* (London: Thompson), pp. 32–43.

Clough, P. and Strycharczyk, D. (2012). Mental Toughness and Its Role in the Development of Young People. In C. van Nieuwerburgh (ed.), *Coaching in Education: Getting Better Results for Students, Educators and Parents* (London: Karnac Books), pp. 75–91.

Clough, P. and Strycharczyk, D. (2014). *Developing Mental Toughness in Young People* (London: Karnac Books).

Coyle, D. (2009). *The Talent Code: Greatness Isn't Born. It's Grown. Here's How* (New York: Bantam).

Coyle, D. (2012). *The Little Book of Talent* (London: Random House).

Crust, L., Earle, K., Perry, J., Earle, F., Clough, A. and Clough, P. (2014). Mental Toughness in Higher Education: Relationships with Achievement and Progression in First-Year University Sports Students. *Personality and Individual Differences* 69: 87–91.

Cuddy, A. (2012). Your Body Language Shapes Who You Are [video]. *TED.com*

References

(June). Available at: https://www.ted.com/talks/amy_cuddy_your_body_language_shapes_who_you_are?language=en.

Cuddy, A., Wilmuth, C. and Carney, D. (2012). The Benefit of Power Posing Before a High-Stakes Social Evaluation. Harvard Business School Working Paper No. 13-027 (September).

Dannemiller, K. D. and Jacobs, R. W. (1992). Changing the Way Organizations Change: A Revolution of Common Sense. *Journal of Applied Behavioural Science* 28(4): 480–498.

Donovan, J. J. and Radosevich, D. J. (1999). A Meta-Analytic Review of the Distribution of Practice Effect: Now You See It, Now You Don't. *Journal of Applied Psychology* 84(5): 795–805.

Doran, G. T. (1981). There's a S.M.A.R.T. Way to Write Management's Goals and Objectives. *Management Review* 70(11): 35–36.

Duckworth, A. L. (2013). The Key to Success? Grit [video]. *TED.com* (April). Available at: https://www.ted.com/talks/angela_lee_duckworth_the_key_to_success_grit?language=en.

Duckworth, A. L., Peterson, C., Matthews, M. D. and Kelly, D. (2007). Grit: Perseverance and Passion for Long-Term Goals. *Journal of Personality and Social Psychology* 92(6): 1087–1101.

Duhigg, C. (2014). *The Power of Habit: Why We Do What We Do in Life and Business* (New York: Random House).

Dweck, C. (1999). *Self Theories: The Role in Motivation, Personality, and Development* (Hove: Psychology Press).

Dweck, C. (2007). *Mindset: The New Psychology of Success* (New York: Ballantine Books).

Ellis, A. (1998). *How to Stubbornly Refuse to Make Yourself Miserable About Anything (Yes, Anything!)* (New York: Citadel Press).

Fan, X., Miller, B. C., Park, K., Winward, B. W., Christensen, M., Grotevant, H. D. and Tai, R. H. (2006). An Exploratory Study About Inaccuracy and Invalidity in Adolescent Self-Report Surveys. *Field Methods* 18: 223–244.

Ferriss, T. (2015) How to Build a Large Audience From Scratch (And More) [podcast], *fourhourworkweek.com* (May). Available at: http://fourhourworkweek.com/2015/05/28/how-to-build-a-large-audience-from-scratch-and-more/.

Ferriss, T. (2007). *The 4-Hour Work Week: Escape the 9–5, Live Anywhere and Join the New Rich* (New York: Crown).

Foer, J. (2012). *Moonwalking with Einstein: The Art and Science of Remembering Everything* (London: Penguin).

Garber, G. (1983). Motivation: Motivational Strategies for Being Organized. *Reading Teacher* 37(2): 217–218.

Gollwitzer, A., Oettingen, G., Kirby, T., Duckworth, A. and Mayer, D. (2011). Mental Contrasting Facilitates Academic Performance in School Children. *Motivation and Emotion* 35: 403–412.

Gollwitzer, P. M. and Bargh, J. A. (eds) (1996). *The Psychology of Action: Linking Cognition and Motivation to Behavior* (New York: Guilford Press).

Kleon, A. (2014). *Show Your Work! 10 Things Nobody Told You About Getting Discovered* (New York: Algonquin Books).

Kübler-Ross, E. (1969). *On Death and Dying* (London: Routledge).

Leitner, S. (2011). *So lernt man lernen* (How We Learn) (Hamburg: Nikol Verlagsgesellschaft mbH).

Lemov, D. (2012). *Practice Perfect: 42 Rules for Getting Better at Getting Better* (New York: Jossey-Bass).

Locke, E. A. and Latham, G. P. (1984). *Goal Setting: A Motivational Technique That Works!* (Englewood Cliffs, NJ: Prentice Hall).

Martin, A. (2010). *Building Classroom Success: Eliminating Academic Fear and Failure* (London: Continuum).

Martin, A. J. and Marsh, H. W. (2009). Academic Resilience and Academic Buoyancy: Multidimensional and Hierarchical Conceptual Framing of Causes, Correlates and Cognate Constructs. *Oxford Review of Education* 35: 353–370.

Maxwell, J. (2012). *Failing Forward: Turning Mistakes into Stepping Stones for Success* (Nashville, TN: Thomas Nelson Publishing).

Miller, G. A. (1956). The Magical Number Seven, Plus or Minus Two: Some Limits On Our Capacity for Processing Information. *Psychological Review* 63: 81–97.

Ntoumanis, N., Healy, C., Sedikides, C., Duda, J., Stewart, B., Smith, A. and Bond, J. (2014). When the Going Gets Tough: The 'Why' of Goal Striving Matters. *Journal of Personality* 82(3): 225–236.

Oettingen, G. (2014). *Rethinking Positive Thinking: Inside the New Science of Motivation* (New York: Penguin).

Palmer, B. (2009). *The Recipe for Success: What Really Successful People Do and How You Can Do it Too* (London: A&C Black).

Pausch, R. with Zaslow, J. (2010). *The Last Lecture* (London: Two Roads).

Peters, S. (2012). *The Chimp Paradox: The Mind Management Programme for Confidence, Success and Happiness* (London: Random House).

References

Putwain, D. W., Nicholson, L. J., Connors, L. and Woods, K. (2013). Resilient Children Are Less Test Anxious and Perform Better in Tests at the End of Primary Schooling. *Learning and Individual Differences* 28: 41–46.

Reason, J. (2013). *A Life in Error: From Little Slips to Big Disasters* (Farnham: Ashgate).

Robbins, A. (1992). *Awaken the Giant Within: How to Take Immediate Control of Your Mental, Emotional, Physical and Financial Life* (New York: Pocket Books).

Rubin, G. (2015). *Better Than Before: Mastering the Habits of Our Everyday Lives* (London: Two Roads).

Snyder, F., Vuchinich, S., Acock, A., Washburn, I. and Flay, B. (2012). Improving Elementary School Quality Through the Use of a Social-Emotional and Character Development Program: A Matched-Pair, Cluster-Randomized, Controlled Trial in Hawai'i. *Journal of School Health* 82(1): 11–20.

St Clair-Thompson, H., Bugler, M., Robinson, J., Clough, P., McGeown, S. P. and Perry, J. (2015). Mental Toughness in Education: Exploring Relationships with Attainment, Attendance, Behavior and Peer Relationships. *Educational Psychology* 35(7): 886–907.

Stafford, T. and Dewar, M. (2014). Tracing the Trajectory of Skill Learning with a Very Large Sample of Online Game Players. *Psychological Science* 25(2): 511–518.

Tough, P. (2013). *How Children Succeed: Grit, Curiosity and the Hidden Power of Character* (London: Random House).

Tracy, B. (2013). *Eat That Frog! Get More of the Important Things Done – Today!* (London: Hodder).

US Department of Education, Office of Educational Technology (2013). *Promoting Grit, Tenacity, and Perseverance: Critical Factors for Success in the 21st Century* (February). Available at: http://pgbovine.net/OET-Draft-Grit-Report-2-17-13.pdf.

Weber, M. and Ruch, W. (2012). The Role of a Good Character in 12 Year Old School Children: Do Character Strengths Matter in the Classroom? *Child Indicators Research* 5: 317–334.

Whitmore, J. (2009). *Coaching for Performance, GROWing Human Potential and Purpose: The Principles and Practice of Coaching and Leadership* (3rd edn) (London: Nicholas Brealey).

Index

Index